BE HEALED

12 Keys To Supernatural Healing

Charles W Morris

Copyright © 2024 Charles W Morris

All rights reserved. No part of this book may be used or reproduced by any means, graphic, electronic, or mechanical, including photocopying, recording, taping, or by any information storage retrieval system without the written permission of the publisher except in the case of brief quotations embodied in critical articles and reviews.

Scriptures are taken from the English Standard Version of the Bible

Books may be ordered through booksellers or by contacting:

RSIP

Raising the Standard International Publishing L. L. C.

https://www.rsipublishing.com

RSIP-Charles Morris
https://www.rsiministry.com
Navarre, Florida

ISBN: 9781960641489
Printed in the United States of America
Edition Date: March 2024

TABLE OF CONTENTS

1	The Complexities Of Healing	1
2	Reasons For Sicknesses, Diseases, Ailments, And Afflictions	5
3	Personal Sins Can Cause Sickness, Illness, Disease. And Death	20
4	Sins Of The Forefathers Can Cause Sickness, Illness, Disease And Death	58
5	Word Curses Can Cause Sickness, Illness, Disease, And Death	74
6	Ungodly Soul Ties Can Cause Sickness, Illness, Disease, And Death	91
7	Demonic Presence In The Way Of Oppression Or Possession Can Cause Sickness, Illness, Disease, And Death	106
8	Word Curses Can Cause Sickness, Illness, Disease, And Death	129
9	Sickness, Illness, Disease, And Death Can Come Upon Us For God's Glory To Be Manifested	140
10	Judgment Of The Flesh For The Purpose Of Reconciliation Can Cause Sickness, Illness, Disease, And Death	143
11	Taking The Lord's Supper In An Unworthy Manner Can Cause Sickness, Illness, Disease, And Death	153

12	Lying To The Holy Spirit Can Cause Sickness, Illness, Disease, And Death	159
13	Unforgiveness Can Cause Sickness, Illness, Disease, And Death	165
14	Reaping What You Sow Can Cause Sickness, Illness, Disease, And Death	187
15	Keys To Follow For Healing	193
	More Books By Charles Morris	
	About The Author	

Chapter 1
THE COMPLEXITIES OF HEALING

Over the course of several years, numerous individuals have approached me, seeking insights into the intricacies of the doctrine of healing. The inquiries I've encountered are diverse, reflecting the complexity of this theological concept. Some common questions that have arisen include:

1. *Temporary Healing and Recurring Sickness:*
Why do certain individuals experience temporary healing only to have the ailment return?

2. *Differential Healing Among People:*
What factors contribute to the healing of some individuals while others do not receive the same outcome?

3. *Life Expectancy Disparities:*
Why is it observed that some seemingly "good" people pass away at a young age, while supposedly "wicked" individuals live long lives?

4. *Limitations of Faith Healers:*
If faith healers possess the ability to heal through faith, why is it that not everyone is healed through their interventions?

5. *The Effectiveness of Faith and Prayers:*
In the face of diseases, why do faith and prayers sometimes appear insufficient to bring about healing for our loved ones?

6. Attribution of Sickness and Afflictions:

There is a profound desire to understand the origins of sickness, diseases, and afflictions. Does sickness and afflictions stem from God, Satan, generational sins, or the personal sins of the afflicted individual?

These questions delve into the complexities of the doctrine of healing, exploring the complex aspects of faith, divine intervention, and the mysteries surrounding the causes and outcomes of physical afflictions. Each inquiry reflects a genuine quest for understanding and meaning in the face of the profound and often perplexing nature of healing within theological frameworks.

Certainly, I want to acknowledge that I don't claim to possess all-encompassing answers to the myriad questions surrounding healing. However, I am eager to share insights drawn from the Scriptures.

To begin, I wholeheartedly embrace the belief in divine supernatural healing, convinced that our heavenly Father desires our well-being and exceeds our expectations in bestowing healing. It's crucial to recognize that the doctrine of healing has, at times, been subject to misuse within various theological perspectives. The convictions I express are not mere personal opinions but are rooted in a Scriptural Doctrine that is accessible and applicable.

A foundational principle is the understanding that we must assess sickness by discerning the possible reasons for its manifestation. Our Lord, as articulated in the Scriptures, claimed to act and speak only in accordance with the Father's guidance. This underscores why He employed diverse healing methods, emphasizing the importance of first consulting the Father before taking any action.

Neglecting this step might lead us to pray against symptoms rather than addressing the root cause of the sickness. Obtaining this knowledge involves prayer and a critical evaluation of our own standing or that of the afflicted before God. It prompts us to consider whether we are in genuine fellowship with the Father, who, in the Scriptures, declared healing over some and cast demons that caused the sickness out of others.

A cautionary note is sounded against the hasty anointing with oil, a quick prayer, and the declaration of a state of healing without first seeking guidance from the Father. This practice, when not grounded in discernment, can inadvertently lead to questioning the faith of the afflicted if healing does not manifest. Therefore, it becomes imperative to seek divine guidance, ensuring that our actions align with the will of the Father. This involves introspection about our fellowship with the Father before engaging in prayers for those manifesting sicknesses.

When Examining An Illness Or Sickness In Someone, It Is Essential To Delve Into A Series Of Probing Questions:

1. *Ancestral Health Patterns:*
Are there common physical issues shared with our ancestors, such as our father or mother?

2. *Lifestyle Choices and Health Impact:*
Have we engaged in a lifestyle that contributes to physical deterioration, such as smoking, drug use, overeating, excessive consumption of sweets, etc.?

3. *Demonic Influence and Activity:*

Charles W Morris

Have we been in contact with individuals influenced by demonic forces, or have we been involved in any form of demonic activity, either before or after salvation?

The imperative to ask these questions is grounded in the principle that, much like our Lord Jesus, who did nothing except in accordance with the Father's guidance, our approach to healing should be discerning. Despite employing various healing methods, Jesus encountered situations where individuals were not healed.

Recognizing the diverse causes of sickness or affliction, our response to each ailment, affliction, or disorder must be tailored accordingly. The Scriptures highlight the uniqueness of Jesus' approach to healing, emphasizing that healings can stem from a simple prayer of faith, the casting out of a demon, or the breaking of a word curse. Hence, seeking God's wisdom and discernment becomes paramount in addressing ailments, afflictions, and sicknesses.

Embarking on a journey through the New Testament, we can study instances where individuals manifested various forms of sickness, ailment, or oppression and observe the distinctive ways in which they were healed. This comprehensive exploration aims to provide an in-depth Scriptural foundation, fostering an understanding of how sicknesses manifest and the potential avenues for healing.

Chapter 2
REASONS FOR SICKNESSES, DISEASES, AILMENTS, AND AFFLICTIONS

Before delving into the reasons behind people experiencing sicknesses, diseases, ailments, and afflictions, it's essential to establish a clear understanding of the term "sickness."

Defining Sickness

Sicknesses, diseases, ailments, and afflictions can be viewed as the absence of health, as defined by the teachings of God's Word. This absence of health encompasses various dimensions:

1. Physical Absence of Health:
Physical ailments like viral or bacterial infections, broken bones, or more severe conditions such as cancer fall under this category.

2. Mental and Emotional Absence of Health:
Issues related to mental and emotional well-being, including anxiety or depression disorders, contribute to the absence of health.

3. Spiritual Absence of Health:
Spiritual dimensions of sickness involve demonic satanic attacks, oppression, possession, or even consequences of God's discipline.

By recognizing these dimensions, we understand that sicknesses, diseases, ailments, and afflictions can manifest on physical, soulish (mental and emotional), or spiritual levels. This comprehensive understanding lays the groundwork for exploring the multifaceted nature of health challenges and the diverse factors contributing to their occurrence.

> *Psalms 119:66-67 (ESV) Teach me good judgment and knowledge, for I believe in your commandments. 67 Before I was afflicted I went astray, but now I keep your word.*
>
> *Psalms 119:71 (ESV) It is good for me that I was afflicted, that I might learn your statutes.*
>
> *Psalms 119:75-77 (ESV) I know, O LORD, that your rules are righteous, and that in faithfulness you have afflicted me. 76 Let your steadfast love comfort me according to your promise to your servant. 77 Let your mercy come to me, that I may live; for your law is my delight.*

Where Does Sickness Come From?

Exploring the origins of sickness, we turn to the rich narrative of the Bible, where the mention of sickness and death emerges very noticeably. According to biblical accounts, the inception of sickness can be traced back to the groundbreaking event of the fall of man, a consequence of the sin and rebellion committed by Adam and Eve.

The pivotal moment is enclosed in Genesis 2:17, where God expressly warned Adam about the repercussions of partaking of the Tree of Knowledge of Good and Evil. In this divine admonition, God conveyed that such an act would result in certain death. It is crucial to note that, before this pivotal event, the concept of death was not a concern for any of God's creations.

The linkage between Adam and Eve's transgression and the introduction of sickness into the world forms a foundational understanding within Biblical teachings. This narrative sets the stage for a comprehensive exploration of the complexities surrounding the existence of sickness and the intricate interplay between human choices, divine consequences, and the broader implications of the fall of man.

> Genesis 2:17 (ESV) but of the tree of the knowledge of good and evil you shall not eat, for in the day that you eat of it you shall surely die."

Upon the pivotal act of consuming the forbidden fruit from the Tree of Knowledge of Good and Evil, Adam and Eve underwent profound spiritual, mental, and physical transformations. The repercussions of this disobedience were manifold.

Firstly, their human spirits experienced a spiritual death, resulting in a profound separation from God. The intimate connection they once enjoyed with the divine was severed, casting a shadow over the spiritual aspect of their existence.

Secondly, the realm of their souls, comprising thoughts, emotions, and choices, became corrupted. This corruption rendered them susceptible to the myriad mental and emotional traumas that afflict individuals today. The once pristine state of their souls was marred, opening the door to the complexities of human suffering.

Lastly, the physical consequence of their disobedience was the imposition of mortality. Their physical bodies, originally formed from the dust of the earth, were now destined to return to that same elemental state. The reality of death became an inevitable fate for their mortal bodies, a stark contrast to the eternal nature they had previously enjoyed.

This narrative provides a detailed yet complex understanding of the profound impact of Adam and Eve's choice on the holistic human experience—spiritually, mentally, and physically. It sets the stage for grappling with the enduring consequences of this pivotal moment in Biblical history.

> *Genesis 3:8 (ESV) And they heard the sound of the LORD God walking in the garden in the cool of the day, and the man and his wife **hid themselves** from the presence of the LORD God among the trees of the garden.*
>
> *Genesis 3:10 (ESV) And he said, "I heard the sound of you in the garden, and **I was afraid**, because I was naked, and I hid myself."*
>
> *Genesis 3:17-19 (ESV) And to Adam he said, "Because you have listened to the voice of your wife and have eaten of the tree of which I commanded you, 'You shall not eat of it,' **cursed is the ground** because of you; **in pain** you shall eat of it all the days of your life; 18 thorns and thistles it shall bring forth for you; and you shall eat the plants of the field. 19 By the sweat of your face you shall eat bread, **till you return to the ground**, for out of it you were taken; for you are dust, and **to dust you shall return**."*
>
> *Romans 5:17 (ESV) For if, because of one man's trespass, death reigned through that one man, much*

more will those who receive the abundance of grace and the free gift of righteousness reign in life through the one man Jesus Christ.

Returning to the fundamental query that looms large—does sickness find its origin in God, Satan, or sin? The Bible offers what appears to be at least three distinct responses to this complex question. In our exploration, we aim to dissect the intricate interplay of sin, the demonic, and God's involvement in the realm of sicknesses, diseases, ailments, and afflictions.

The Biblical Relationship Between Sin And Sickness

In the upcoming Chapter 3, aptly titled "Personal Sins Can Cause Sickness, Illness, Disease, And Death," we delve into the Biblical narrative that explains the profound connection between individual sins and the manifestation of sickness. This exploration will shed light on how personal choices can serve as precursors to health challenges.

The Biblical Relationship Between Satan And Sickness

Chapter 7, titled "Demonic Presence In The Way Of Oppression Or Possession Can Cause Sickness, Illness, Disease, And Death," is dedicated to unraveling the Biblical discourse on the link between the demonic realm and the afflictions experienced by individuals. This examination will bring to the forefront the potential influence of demonic forces on health outcomes.

God's Role in Sicknesses, Diseases, Ailments, and Afflictions

The multifaceted role of God in the context of sicknesses will be scrutinized in Chapters 9 through 11. Here, we anticipate a distinctive exploration of how divine intervention, purpose, and sovereignty intersect with the complex tapestry of health challenges.

This structured approach aims to provide a comprehensive understanding of the Biblical perspectives on the origins of sickness, allowing for an in-depth exploration of sin, the demonic, and God's intricate involvement in the intricate dynamics of human health.

God And Sickness

The Scriptures provide a wealth of examples that underscore the correlation between adherence to the Old Testament Law and the consequences of sicknesses, diseases, ailments, afflictions, and even death—both for nations outside the covenant and God's own people. This connection is notably evident in instances where God utilized these afflictions as instruments of judgment, serving as punitive measures for disobedience.

Underlining the gravity of disobedience, God explicitly warned His people about the impending diseases that would befall them due to their continual defiance of His commands. Deuteronomy 28:1-14 serves as a piercing passage wherein God outlines the blessings that will be bestowed upon His people if they adhere faithfully to His commands. Conversely, Deuteronomy 28:15-68 forewarns of the curses that will befall the disobedient—a comprehensive catalog of afflictions, including specific diseases.

In these passages, God not only articulates the consequences but also describes the types of diseases that would afflict those who rebel against His divine instructions.

BE HEALED

The meticulous detailing in Deuteronomy offers a profound insight into the divine governance of health outcomes based on obedience or disobedience. This intricate interplay between divine consequences and human actions is a recurring theme in the Old Testament, illustrating the gravity and range of the consequences tied to adherence or deviation from God's commands.

> *Deuteronomy 28:22 (ESV) The LORD will strike you with wasting disease and with fever, inflammation and fiery heat, and with drought and with blight and with mildew. They shall pursue you until you perish.*

The intricate dynamics between disobedience and the resultant afflictions, particularly sicknesses and diseases, manifest as a recurrent theme in Biblical narratives. It becomes evident that God, in response to the disobedience of His people, not only allowed but actively released afflictions to impact them. Several instances within the Scriptures underscore this profound connection, highlighting God's role in permitting these afflictions as consequences for sin, rebellion, and disobedience.

Delving further into the Biblical tapestry, we encounter additional examples where God, as an settler of divine justice, sanctioned the release of sicknesses, diseases, ailments, and afflictions upon His people. These instances stand as stark illustrations of the consequential relationship between human transgressions and the divine response.

In examining these Biblical accounts, we gain deeper insights into the nature of divine governance, where afflictions are not merely passive outcomes but deliberate actions allowed by God. The interplay between human choices and divine consequences unfolds as a compelling narrative, emphasizing the gravity of disobedience and the corresponding measures enacted by a just and sovereign God.

> *Exodus 4:11 (ESV) Then the LORD said to him, "Who has made man's mouth? Who makes him mute, or deaf, or seeing, or blind? **Is it not I, the LORD**?*
>
> *Ezekiel 3:26 (ESV) And I will make your tongue cling to the roof of your mouth, so that **you shall be mute** and unable to reprove them, for they are a rebellious house.*
>
> *Luke 1:18-20 (ESV) And Zechariah said to the angel, "How shall I know this? For I am an old man, and my wife is advanced in years." 19 And the angel answered him, "I am Gabriel. I stand in the presence of God, and I was sent to speak to you and to bring you this good news. 20 And behold, **you will be silent and unable to speak** until the day that these things take place, because you did not believe my words, which will be fulfilled in their time."*
>
> *Amos 3:6-7 (ESV) Is a trumpet blown in a city, and the people are not afraid? Does disaster come to a city, **unless the LORD has done it**? 7 "For the Lord GOD does nothing without revealing his secret to his servants the prophets.*
>
> *Exodus 15:26 (ESV) saying, "If you will diligently listen to the voice of the LORD your God, and do that which is right in his eyes, and give ear to his commandments and keep all his statutes, **I will put none of the diseases on you that I put on the Egyptians**, for I am the LORD, your healer."*

BE HEALED

*Exodus 12:29 (ESV) At midnight **the LORD struck down all the firstborn in the land** of Egypt, from the firstborn of Pharaoh who sat on his throne to the firstborn of the captive who was in the dungeon, and all the firstborn of the livestock.*

*Deuteronomy 7:15 (ESV) And the LORD will take away from you all sickness, and none of the evil diseases of Egypt, which you knew, will he inflict on you, but **he will lay them on all who hate you**.*

*Deuteronomy 28:60 (ESV) And **he will bring upon you again all the diseases of Egypt**, of which you were afraid, and they shall cling to you.*

*Numbers 11:33 (ESV) While the meat was yet between their teeth, before it was consumed, the anger of the LORD was kindled against the people, and **the LORD struck down the people with a very great plague**.*

*2 Kings 15:5 (ESV) And **the LORD touched the king, so that he was a leper** to the day of his death, and he lived in a separate house. And Jotham the king's son was over the household, governing the people of the land.*

*2 Chronicles 21:14-15 (ESV) behold, **the LORD will bring a great plague on your people**, your children, your wives, and all your possessions, 15 and you yourself will have **a severe sickness with a disease of your bowels**, until your bowels come out because of the disease, day by day.'"*

*Isaiah 10:16 (ESV) Therefore **the Lord GOD of hosts will send wasting sickness** among his stout*

> warriors, and under his glory a burning will be kindled, like the burning of fire.

What Is Divine Healing?

> Acts 10:38 (ESV) how God anointed Jesus of Nazareth with the Holy Spirit and with power. He went about doing good and healing all who were oppressed by the devil, for God was with him.

Supernatural divine healing represents a profound and comprehensive restoration of health, addressing sicknesses, diseases, ailments, and afflictions through the atoning work of our Lord Jesus Christ. While the understanding of this concept is inherent, it's essential to emphasize that for an intervention to be classified as supernatural divine healing, it necessitates a direct and explicit interaction from God. This distinction is crucial, as divine healing operates beyond the realm of natural laws governing health recovery through conventional methods such as medicine or surgery.

Distinct from approaches grounded in natural means, divine healing is characterized by its intrinsic association with the supernatural— an intervention that transcends the ordinary and can only be ascribed to the touch of God the Father. It extends beyond mere positive confession, wishful thinking, or a generic prayer of faith. The term "divine healing" encompasses a depth that resonates with a supernatural component, underscoring the involvement of our Lord Jesus Christ and the power of the Holy Spirit in the restoration of health.

Biblical narratives, spanning both the Old and New Testaments, abound with instances of divine healing. Within these accounts, diverse methods are employed, showcasing the multifaceted nature of divine intervention in the healing process. While the prayer of faith, as articulated in James 5:13-16, holds significance and will be explored more extensively in later discussions, it serves as one facet within the broader spectrum of divine healing methods documented in the Scriptures.

> *James 5:13-16 (ESV) Is anyone among you suffering? Let him pray. Is anyone cheerful? Let him sing praise. 14 Is anyone among you sick? Let him call for the elders of the church, and let them pray over him, anointing him with oil in the name of the Lord. 15 And the prayer of faith will save the one who is sick, and the Lord will raise him up. And if he has committed sins, he will be forgiven. 16 Therefore, confess your sins to one another and pray for one another, that you may be healed. The prayer of a righteous person has great power as it is working.*

Within the Christian community, there is a prevalent desire for the "gift of healing" and a shared aspiration to witness regular healing through prayer. Yet, in our pursuit of healing, it is equally essential to inquire into the reasons behind the continual occurrence of sicknesses and illnesses. Additionally, we must grapple with the observation that, at times, the relief individuals experience from prayer seems to be complemented by medical treatments prescribed by doctors. To unravel these complexities, let us first delve into the reasons underlying the affliction of sicknesses and diseases and explore effective prayer strategies for healing.

Drawing from the Scriptures, I will list various factors that, according to biblical accounts, serve as doorways to sickness, disease, affliction, and even death. Following this examination, we will scrutinize instances of healing, exploring the methods employed and whose faith was instrumental in the restoration process.

Crucially, in addressing these reasons for ailments, whether a person is saved or not becomes a secondary consideration. What emerges as pivotal is the individual's knowledge of or relationship with the Lord Jesus Christ, as these factors often determine the pathway to healing. It is noteworthy that healing from these afflictions is sometimes intricately linked to the intercession of others pleading before the Lord on behalf of the afflicted.

Reflecting on the Word of God, we witness instances where our Lord Jesus Christ, endowed with all nine spiritual gifts of the Holy Spirit, manifested healing through various means. At times, it appeared that our Lord would manifest His presence, and healing would unfold seemingly spontaneously through a mere spoken word.

His supernatural spiritual gifts included faith, words of knowledge, words of wisdom, prophecy, gifts of healing, working of miracles, and discernment of spirits. These supernatural gifts enabled Him to discern the underlying root issues behind visible symptoms, going beyond the notion that all ailments result solely from old age or hereditary factors.

In unraveling the intricate dynamics of healing, it becomes apparent that our Lord's interventions were not arbitrary but were driven by a deep understanding of the spiritual realm and a profound connection with the needs of each individual. This exploration serves as a foundation for comprehending the multifaceted nature of healing within the Christian faith.

> *1 Corinthians 12:8-10 (ESV) For to one is given through the Spirit the **utterance of wisdom**, and to another the **utterance of knowledge** according to the*

> *same Spirit, 9 to another **faith** by the same Spirit, to another **gifts of healing** by the one Spirit, 10 to another the **working of miracles**, to another **prophecy**, to another the **ability to distinguish between spirits,** to another **various kinds of tongues**, to another **the interpretation of tongues**.*

Let's delve into the examination of twelve distinct ways through which sickness, illness, disease, and even death can manifest, drawing on Biblical examples for each scenario. By scrutinizing these instances in detail, we aim to gain a comprehensive understanding of the diverse factors contributing to health challenges and the corresponding methods employed for healing.

Upon discerning the underlying reasons behind sickness, illness, or disease, the Lord Jesus Christ demonstrated a dynamic approach to bring about healing. His methods served as a model, highlighting that praying for someone's healing is not intended to follow a one-size-fits-all methodology. In some cases, He cast out demons, while in others, He laid His hands on the afflicted. Our Lord also spoke words of faith and acknowledged the faith of others as instrumental in the healing process.

This exploration into various healing methods opens the door for us to cultivate a deeper understanding of the spiritual aspects involved in praying for the healing of others. It challenges the notion of passive and powerless prayer meetings, where wishful thinking and reliance on medical science and time for a "speedy" recovery have become prevalent. The recognition that a natural course of recovery, like a cold running its course in seven to ten days, does not align with the biblical concept of healing prompts us to reassess our approach.

Charles W Morris

While personally acknowledging the invaluable contributions of medical personnel, treatments, and medications, it is crucial to differentiate between scientific and medical interventions, classified in the natural or fleshly realm, and Biblical healing, situated in the supernatural or spiritual realm. This distinction underscores the unique and profound nature of divine intervention in the healing process, elevating our understanding beyond conventional approaches to health and well-being.

1. *Personal Sins Can Cause Sickness, Illness, Disease. And Death.*
2. *Sins Of The Forefathers Can Cause Sickness, Illness, Disease And Death.*
3. *Word Curses Can Cause Sickness, Illness, Disease, And Death.*
4. *Ungodly Soul Ties Can Cause Sickness, Illness, Disease, And Death.*
5. *Demonic Presence In Way Of Oppression Or Possession Can Cause Sickness, Illness, Disease, And Death.*
6. *Natural Law Of Sin And Death Can Cause Sickness, Illness, Disease And Death.*
7. *Sickness, Illness, Disease, And Death Can Come Upon Us For God's Glory To Be Manifested.*
8. *Judgment Of The Flesh For The Purpose Of Reconciliation Can Cause Sickness, Illness, Disease, And Death.*
9. *Taking The Lord's Supper In An Unworthy Manner Can Cause Sickness, Illness, Disease, And Death.*
10. *Lying To The Holy Spirit Can Cause Sickness, Illness, Disease, And Death.*
11. *Unforgiveness Can Cause Sickness, Illness, Disease, And Death.*

12. Reaping What You Sow Can Cause Sickness, Illness, Disease, And Death.

Now, let's meticulously analyze the intricacies surrounding the onset of sickness, disease, ailments, and afflictions, along with the corresponding methods employed by Jesus or His followers for healing. The ensuing chapters will present an array of Scriptures, emphasizing that the compilation is by no means exhaustive but serves as a comprehensive and thorough analysis of the subject.

Chapter 3
PERSONAL SINS CAN CAUSE SICKNESS, ILLNESS, DISEASE. AND DEATH

Despite being saved and having the indwelling presence of the Holy Spirit within us, it is crucial to acknowledge that we, as individuals, retain a fallen nature. While it may not be our expectation, the reality is that we will inevitably, at times, succumb to sin. This recognition underscores the ongoing tension between our redeemed state and the lingering effects of our fallen human nature. It serves as a reminder of the continual need for grace, repentance, and reliance on the transformative power of the Holy Spirit in our journey of faith.

This chapter will stand as one of the lengthiest sections in the book, yet it holds paramount significance as we establish a critical link between the repercussions of our daily decisions and the onset of afflictions and illnesses. So, hang in there as you read.

Sin And Sickness

The question of whether all sicknesses, illnesses, diseases, ailments, and death stem from God due to sin is multifaceted. Firstly, in a broader theological sense, one can affirm that, yes, if Adam and Eve had not succumbed to sin, the existence of sickness and death would not have manifested. The origin of all illnesses and deaths can be traced back to the foundational sin committed by Adam and Eve.

However, delving into a more nuanced perspective, the answer becomes more intricate. Drawing insights from Scriptures, particularly John 9, it becomes evident that not every instance of sickness is a direct consequence of personal sins. There are cases where illnesses are not brought about by God in response to specific sins committed by individuals.

Yet, it is crucial to recognize that sin can still be a contributing factor to sickness, albeit not as a direct divine punishment. Instances such as the disease of AIDS resulting from sexual sins, cancer stemming from years of smoking, or high blood pressure due to obesity exemplify how sinful behaviors can lead to adverse health conditions. Additionally, psychological conditions like anxiety or depression can also contribute to illness, affecting both the mind and the body.

In navigating this complex relationship between sin and sickness, it is important to appreciate the balance between acknowledging the overarching impact of the original sin on human existence and recognizing the indirect influence of personal choices on health outcomes. This distinctive perspective allows for a more comprehensive understanding of the intricate interplay between sin, sickness, and the broader human experience.

Various perspectives exist regarding the connection between sickness and sin. One perspective suggests that there may be an assumption that hidden sin, deeply embedded in the mind or a person's history, could be the root cause of their health issues. This viewpoint seeks to explain the lack of health by attributing it to some undisclosed transgressions within the individual.

Another viewpoint takes a different approach, categorizing all sicknesses as indicative of a lack of faith on the part of the afflicted person, effectively framing the state of illness as a manifestation of sin. According to this perspective, the absence of healing is seen as a consequence of the person's perceived deficiency in faith.

Some individuals attribute the persistence of sickness to specific sins, positing that people fail to recover from their ailments due to ongoing transgressions. Additionally, there is a belief that an absence of healing can be linked to unconfessed sin, and admitting to physical symptoms is viewed as a "negative confession" that hinders the prospect of healing.

On the contrary, there are those who argue that it is incorrect for individuals to bear diseases in their bodies, citing the prophetic Word concerning Jesus, which states that He bore our griefs, and, through His stripes, we are healed. This perspective emphasizes the redemptive power of Christ's sacrifice and questions the acceptance of diseases in light of this Biblical promise.

In examining these diverse viewpoints, it becomes apparent that interpretations vary widely, ranging from associating sickness with hidden sins or lack of faith to questioning the legitimacy of bearing diseases in the context of Biblical promises. The intersection of theology, belief systems, and personal experiences shapes the intricate tapestry of perspectives surrounding the relationship between sin and sickness. We will break it down using only the Word of God as our authoritative source.

> *Isaiah 53:4-5 (ESV) Surely he has borne our griefs and carried our sorrows; yet we esteemed him stricken, smitten by God, and afflicted. 5 But he was pierced for our transgressions; he was crushed for our iniquities; upon him was the chastisement that*

brought us peace, and with his wounds we are healed.

Individuals who assert that a Christian's lack of healing is a consequence of being outside of God's will, attributed to either unbelief or sin, often hastily misquote Matthew 9:2. It is essential to scrutinize this claim and also consider the context of James 5:15 for a more comprehensive understanding.

Matthew 9:2 is sometimes invoked to support the idea that an unhealed Christian is inherently linked to personal failings such as unbelief or sin. However, a closer examination of the verse reveals a pointed situation where Jesus not only forgives the paralyzed man's sins but also heals him. This challenges the simplistic notion that all instances of unhealed conditions are a direct result of personal shortcomings.

Turning to James 5:15 provides further insight into the relationship between faith and healing. This passage encourages the prayer of faith for the sick, indicating that healing can be connected to faith. However, it doesn't exclusively attribute illness to unbelief or sin. Instead, it underscores the potential efficacy of fervent prayer rooted in faith.

By critically examining these verses, it becomes apparent that a blanket assertion tying lack of healing to unbelief or sin oversimplifies the complexities inherent in the Christian understanding of health and faith. Both Matthew 9:2 and James 5:15 invite a distinct interpretation that acknowledges the multifaceted dynamics at play in the intersection of faith, healing, and God's will.

Matthew 9:2 (ESV) And behold, some people brought to him a paralytic, lying on a bed. And when Jesus saw their faith, he said to the paralytic, "Take heart, my son; your sins are forgiven."

James 5:15 (ESV) And the prayer of faith will save the one who is sick, and the Lord will raise him up. And if he has committed sins, he will be forgiven.

What often goes unnoticed in this discussion is the paramount importance God places on spiritual healing, recognizing its significance for our eternal destiny. The notion presented raises a thought-provoking question: Would Jesus heal someone physically and then declare, "Your physical ailment is gone, but unfortunately, your soul remains unhealed, leading to eternal condemnation"? Of course not! This rhetorical question asserts that such a scenario is inconceivable. The underlying principle here is that spiritual healing is unequivocally more crucial, emphasizing that both physical and spiritual healing are intertwined. It is asserted that Jesus doesn't selectively address one aspect without considering the other; rather, the two forms of healing are interconnected.

Drawing your attention back to James 5:15, the inclusion of the phrase "...and if he has committed any sins" reflects an acknowledgment that the concept of sin is part of the broader context of healing. However, it does not exclusively attribute sickness to sin, and the emphasis remains on the significance of faith in the healing process.

Exploring Hebrews 12:6-9 introduces the idea of God's discipline, likening it to the discipline administered by earthly fathers. The analogy prompts a reflection on whether a loving earthly parent would ever impose sickness as a form of punishment on their children. The conclusion drawn is a resounding rejection of such an idea, extending the reasoning to question whether our compassionate heavenly Father would inflict sickness as a means of discipline.

In essence, the presented perspective challenges the notion that physical ailments are a direct consequence of spiritual failings. It emphasizes the interconnectedness of spiritual and physical healing, aligning with the understanding that God's primary concern is our spiritual well-being, coupled with a compassionate and disciplined approach that doesn't involve punitive infliction of sickness.

> *Hebrews 12:5-11 (ESV) And have you forgotten the exhortation that addresses you as sons? "My son, do not regard lightly the discipline of the Lord, nor be weary when reproved by him. 6 For the Lord disciplines the one he loves, and chastises every son whom he receives." 7 It is for discipline that you have to endure. God is treating you as sons. For what son is there whom his father does not discipline? 8 If you are left without discipline, in which all have participated, then you are illegitimate children and not sons. 9 Besides this, we have had earthly fathers who disciplined us and we respected them. Shall we not much more be subject to the Father of spirits and live? 10 For they disciplined us for a short time as it seemed best to them, but he disciplines us for our good, that we may share his holiness. 11 For the moment all discipline seems painful rather than pleasant, but later it yields the peaceful fruit of righteousness to those who have been trained by it.*

Consider the scenario: if God were to inflict sickness upon us as a direct consequence of our sins, even under His grace, His undeserved favor, then it follows logically that all Christians would consistently be in a state of illness. Which sin would bring the sickness? How many times must I be guilty of the transgression before punitive judgment? However, adopting a Biblical perspective invites a refined understanding, reminding us that not every instance of sickness can be attributed to sin.

When we assert that sin has the potential to cause sickness, illness, and disease, it becomes imperative to delve into the fundamental questions of "What is sin?" and "When did it enter mankind?" A prevalent contemporary view tends to define sin subjectively, based on individual perspectives of right and wrong. However, to truly comprehend sin, it is essential to approach it through the lens of our Lord's perspective. The roots of sin trace back to Adam and Eve's disobedience to God, marking the initial occurrence of sin in human history. Simply put, sin is transgression against God's commands and character.

Sin Is Transgression Against God's Commands

> *1 John 3:4 (ESV) Everyone who makes a practice of sinning also practices lawlessness; sin is lawlessness.*

Sin Entered Mankind Through Adam And Eve's Rebellion And Disobedience

> *Romans 5:12 (ESV) Therefore, just as sin came into the world through one man, and death through sin, and so death spread to all men because all sinned—*
>
> *Romans 5:18-19 (ESV) Therefore, as one trespass led to condemnation for all men, so one act of righteousness leads to justification and life for all men. 19 For as by the one man's disobedience the many*

were made sinners, so by the one man's obedience the many will be made righteous.

All Mankind Is Guilty Of Being Sinners

God the Father observed that the core of humanity was deeply entrenched in sin, thus veering towards evil. This observation indicates a fundamental understanding within the Christian tradition that human nature is sinful. The statement resonates with a Biblical perspective that highlights the pervasive nature of human depravity.

Scripture underscores the notion that human hearts are inherently inclined towards sinful behavior. It echoes the sentiment that there is no individual who can be deemed righteous or good by their own merit. This principle finds expression in passages such as Romans 3:10, which asserts, "There is no one righteous, not even one."

The exception to this pervasive state of moral corruption is identified in Jesus Christ, who, according to the Word of God, exemplifies perfect righteousness and goodness. In contrast to the fallen nature of humanity, Jesus embodies divine purity and serves as the ultimate standard of goodness because He was without sin.

Therefore, the acknowledgment of human depravity underscores the need for redemption and salvation, which is made possible through the grace and atoning sacrifice of Jesus Christ. It serves as a reminder of humanity's inherent brokenness and the reliance on divine intervention for restoration and reconciliation with God.

Genesis 6:5 (ESV) The LORD saw that the wickedness of man was great in the earth, and that every intention of the thoughts of his heart was only evil continually.

Jeremiah 17:9 (ESV) The heart is deceitful above all things, and desperately sick; who can understand it?

Romans 3:10-18 (ESV) as it is written: "None is righteous, no, not one; 11 no one understands; no one seeks for God. 12 All have turned aside; together they have become worthless; no one does good, not even one." 13 "Their throat is an open grave; they use their tongues to deceive." "The venom of asps is under their lips." 14 "Their mouth is full of curses and bitterness." 15 "Their feet are swift to shed blood; 16 in their paths are ruin and misery, 17 and the way of peace they have not known." 18 "There is no fear of God before their eyes."

Luke 18:18-19 (ESV) And a ruler asked him, "Good Teacher, what must I do to inherit eternal life?" 19 And Jesus said to him, "Why do you call me good? No one is good except God alone.

Some Will Attempt Another Gospel To Deal With The Sin Issue

The pervasive nature of deception prompts certain individuals to substitute Christ with what the Bible terms as "another Jesus and another gospel." This deceptive maneuver is driven by the misguided notion that an alternative path can effectively address the profound issue of sin.

In the quest to mitigate the impact of sin, some individuals fall prey to the allure of false teachings that masquerade as authentic expressions of Biblical truth. These counterfeit messages often contain elements of truth, which make them all the more deceptive and appealing to unsuspecting ears.

However, it is crucial to recognize that accepting such false doctrines, even if they contain fragments of Biblical truth, constitutes a grave error. It represents a departure from the genuine message of salvation and redemption that is exclusively found in Christ.

The danger lies in succumbing to the temptation of embracing teachings that deviate from the authentic Gospel. By doing so, individuals risk compromising the integrity of their faith and jeopardizing their spiritual well-being.

Therefore, discernment is paramount in distinguishing between the genuine Gospel of Christ and counterfeit ideologies that seek to distort the truth. It is imperative to remain steadfast in adherence to the unadulterated message of salvation through Christ alone, guarding against the subtle allure of deceptive doctrines that lead astray from the path of righteousness.

> *2 Corinthians 11:3-4 (ESV) But I am afraid that as the serpent deceived Eve by his cunning, your thoughts will be led astray from a sincere and pure devotion to Christ. 4 For if someone comes and proclaims another Jesus than the one we proclaimed, or if you receive a different spirit from the one you received, or if you accept a different gospel from the one you accepted, you put up with it readily enough.*
>
> *Galatians 1:6-9 (ESV) I am astonished that you are so quickly deserting him who called you in the grace of Christ and are turning to a different gospel— 7 not that there is another one, but there are some who trouble you and want to distort the gospel of Christ. 8 But even if we or an angel from heaven should preach*

> *to you a gospel contrary to the one we preached to you, let him be accursed. 9 As we have said before, so now I say again: If anyone is preaching to you a gospel contrary to the one you received, let him be accursed.*

If We Say We Have No Sin, We Are Deceived

Sin permeates every facet of human existence, affecting all individuals without exception. Throughout history, no human being has been immune to its grasp, save for our Lord Jesus Christ. Sin manifests itself in the rupture of the intimate relationship and fellowship between humanity and God, a consequence that reverberates throughout creation.

Before the redemptive work of Jesus Christ, humanity languished in bondage to sin, held captive by the powers of darkness. We were estranged from what our true identity should be as children of the Most High God, if we receive Christ as our Savior. Otherwise, being spiritually lost meant our allegiance was to a realm of spiritual enslavement, far removed from the divine inheritance ordained for us.

It was through the sacrificial act of Jesus Christ, culminating in His death on the cross and subsequent resurrection, that liberation was bestowed upon humanity by faith in our Lord's finished work. Through His triumph over sin and death, Christ inaugurated a new covenant, enabling the Spirit of adoption to emancipate us from the bondage of sin and reconcile us to our rightful status as sons and daughters of God.

This transformation is not wrought by human effort or merit but is conferred upon us through faith in the completed work of Jesus Christ on the cross. Through His atoning sacrifice, the barriers of sin are shattered, and the pathway to restoration and reconciliation with God is paved. Thus, by embracing the effectiveness of Christ's redemptive act, by faith anyone who believes is adopted into the position of divine favor and sonship and ushered into communion with the Most High God.

> *1 John 1:8 (ESV) If we say we have no sin, we deceive ourselves, and the truth is not in us.*

The Bible unequivocally rejects the notion of categorizing sin into "Big Sin-Little Sin." According to its teachings, every transgression against the Word and character of God constitutes sin, regardless of its perceived magnitude. Sin, in its essence, represents a violation of God's divine standards and a departure from His righteous character.

While all sins share the common trait of defying God's will and commandments, the repercussions and consequences they entail can vary significantly. Certain transgressions may result in more profound and enduring effects than others, shaping the course of our lives in profound ways.

Engaging in personal sins involves a direct defiance of the holiness inherent in God's nature. As explained in Galatians 5:22-23, the character of God exemplifies attributes such as love, joy, peace, patience, kindness, goodness, faithfulness, gentleness, and self-control. Any deviation from these qualities constitutes a departure from the divine standard and an affront to God's sovereignty.

Furthermore, our sinful actions represent a rebellion against the will of God as articulated in His Word. The Scriptures serve as a moral compass, guiding believers towards righteous living and obedience to God's precepts.

When we deviate from these guidelines, we rebel against the very essence of God's revealed truth.

In essence, sin is synonymous with rebellion against God, akin to an act of witchcraft in its defiance of divine authority. By choosing to walk in disobedience, we not only oppose God's commands but also undermine His sovereign rule over our lives.

Therefore, the gravity of sin lies not merely in its outward manifestation but in its fundamental defiance of God's nature, will, and Word. As believers, we are called to strive for holiness and righteousness, aligning our lives with the divine principles laid out in Scripture, and seeking forgiveness and restoration through the redeeming grace of Jesus Christ. Those who walk in the Spirit will not fulfill the deeds of the flesh.

> *1 Samuel 15:22-24 (ESV) And Samuel said, "Has the LORD as great delight in burnt offerings and sacrifices, as in obeying the voice of the LORD? Behold, to obey is better than sacrifice, and to listen than the fat of rams. 23 For rebellion is as the sin of divination, and presumption is as iniquity and idolatry. Because you have rejected the word of the LORD, he has also rejected you from being king." 24 Saul said to Samuel, "I have sinned, for I have transgressed the commandment of the LORD and your words, because I feared the people and obeyed their voice.*

> *Galatians 5:16 (ESV) But I say, walk by the Spirit, and you will not gratify the desires of the flesh.*

As we conclude our reflection on the universal reality of human sinfulness, rooted in the inherent Adamic nature inherited by all humanity, it is essential to underscore this foundational truth with insights gleaned from Scripture. The Scriptures provide profound insights into the nature of sin and its far-reaching consequences, guiding us towards a deeper understanding of our need for salvation.

First and foremost, Scripture unequivocally affirms the universality of human sinfulness, tracing its origins back to the fall of Adam and Eve in the Garden of Eden. Through their disobedience, sin entered the world, tainting the entirety of human existence and predisposing every individual to its pervasive influence. As descendants of Adam, we inherit not only the physical traits but also the spiritual legacy of his sinful nature.

Moreover, Scripture highlights the dire consequences of sin, both in the temporal and eternal realms. Sin broke the harmonious relationship between man and God, erecting barriers that separate us from His presence and fellowship. Its corrosive effects penetrate every aspect of human experience, leading to brokenness, suffering, sickness, death, and spiritual alienation from God.

The Scriptures also emphasize the moral blame and responsibility inherent in human sinfulness, holding each individual accountable for their thoughts, words, and actions. Despite our best efforts, we fall short of God's perfect standard, succumbing to the allure of sin and yielding to its destructive power. This acknowledgment of our sinful condition serves as a motivation for humility and repentance, prompting us to turn to God in contrition and seek His forgiveness and redemption.

In light of the profound truths illuminated by Scripture, we are compelled to confront the reality of our sinful nature and acknowledge our need for salvation and forgiveness. Salvation, as revealed in Scripture, is not merely a theoretical concept but a transformative reality made possible through the sacrificial death and resurrection of Jesus Christ. Through His atoning work on the cross, Christ offers forgiveness for our sins, reconciliation with God, and the promise of eternal life to all who place their faith in Him.

Therefore, as we contemplate the sobering realities of sin and its consequences, let us humbly embrace the hope and redemption offered through Christ, acknowledging our need for His saving grace and surrendering our lives to His transformative power. In doing so, we find assurance of forgiveness, restoration, and eternal fellowship with the One who loves us unconditionally and offers us the gift of salvation.

1. *We were born with a sinful nature. Therefore, all men have the seed nature to sin.*
2. *Sin is rebellion against the holiness and sovereign will of God.*
3. *Sin is a condition of the spirit, soul, and body which manifests practically in words, deeds, and thoughts.*
4. *The wages of sin is death. Those who die physically in their sins have died a spiritual, soulish, and physical death.*
5. *The root of sin is in the human heart.*
6. *Each man is individually accountable for his sin.*
7. *Our Lord Jesus Christ and His work on the cross can redeem us from the penalty and power of sin in our lives.*
8. *We receive salvation by faith. Call on the name of Jesus.*

We are not an island unto ourselves. As individuals, we exist within a complex web of relationships and responsibilities, and as believers, we are called to recognize that our choices carry significant weight beyond our own

BE HEALED

personal desires. The notion of "having it our way" or acting solely according to our own whims is directly opposed to the principles of stewardship and community that characterize the Christian life.

Every decision we make, whether trivial or substantial, has ripple effects that extend far beyond the immediate moment. Our choices resonate spiritually, emotionally, relationally, financially, and physically, shaping our lives and impacting those around us.

Many of us love coffee so I'll use it as an illustration. Consider, for instance, the seemingly innocent decision to purchase a $6 cup of coffee each morning on the way to work. While this expenditure may appear inconsequential by itself, its cumulative effect becomes apparent when viewed through the lens of broader financial stewardship. A weekly expense of $30 translates to $120 per month, a sum that could significantly contribute to the financial well-being of a family, particularly if resources are limited.

In the context of a marital relationship, such decisions can amplify existing tensions and strain the fabric of trust and communication. Imagine a scenario where one spouse, perhaps unaware of the financial implications, continues to indulge in this daily expense, while the other, fully aware of the broader financial responsibilities, expresses concern. What begins as a seemingly trivial disagreement over coffee expenditure can escalate into a larger conflict, fueled by underlying issues of financial management, communication, and mutual respect.

As tensions escalate, the once-harmonious dynamics within the family unit may deteriorate, giving way to bitterness, resentment, and emotional distance. What started as a solitary decision made each morning now reverberates throughout the family structure, influencing all other interactions and decisions.

It is imperative for believers to exercise discernment and mindfulness in their decision-making processes, recognizing the interconnectedness of their choices and the potential ramifications they entail. By prioritizing stewardship, communication, and mutual respect within relationships, believers can navigate challenges with grace and integrity. This will foster an environment conducive to growth and unity. Ultimately, our commitment to honoring God in all aspects of life, including our daily choices, serves as a testament to our faith and commitment to living in accordance with His will.

Let's Look At A Biblical Example: The Blind Man

In examining a Biblical example found in John 9, we encounter a profound interaction between Jesus and His disciples regarding the case of a man born blind. The disciples, grappling with the theological implications of human suffering, posed a question to Jesus, seeking clarity on the origin of the man's blindness.

Their inquiry stemmed from a commonly known doctrine that some physical afflictions such as blindness were directly linked to personal or generational sins. This prevailing understanding reflected a viewpoint that the judgment of God over sin was the explanation for human suffering and misfortune. The disciples, influenced by this doctrinal teaching, sought to discern the cause behind the man's condition.

Their question narrowed the perspective of possible explanations to the man's blindness to two primary factors. Either the man himself had committed sin, leading to his affliction, or the blindness was a consequence of his parents' transgressions. In their attempt to grapple with the complexities of suffering and sin, the disciples unwittingly imposed their neat explanation of why people are afflicted within the confines of their theological understanding.

Jesus' response to the disciples' inquiry in the narrative of the blind man challenges the limitations of their simplistic interpretation, constrained by human logic and conventional theological wisdom. While acknowledging the prevailing theological doctrine that sins could indeed lead to afflictions such as blindness, Jesus redirects their focus by asserting that their understanding of this particular case is flawed.

Our Lord redirects the discourse surrounding the man's blindness, turning the focus away from assigning blame and towards a deeper revelation of God's redemptive purpose. Jesus declares that neither the man nor his parents' sin caused his blindness, but rather, his condition serves as an opportunity for the manifestation of God's glory.

Our Lord Jesus Christ does not dismiss the theological premise that sins can result in physical ailments such as blindness. Jesus' response challenges their simplistic interpretation limited by human logic and conventional wisdom. He did not tell them they were wrong about their theological beliefs that sins can cause afflictions such as blindness. He told them they were wrong about this case.

He invites the disciples to reconsider their application of this belief in the context of the blind man's situation. By doing so, Jesus challenges the disciples to expand their rigid theological framework and embrace a more kingdom understanding of divine providence and redemptive purpose.

In highlighting the uniqueness of the blind man's circumstances, Jesus underscores the complexity of human suffering and the Father's desire for divine intervention in the lives of mankind. In this case, instead of attributing the man's blindness to a specific sin—whether committed by him or his parents, our Lord Jesus emphasized the transformative potential resulting in seeing the Father glorified.

By challenging the disciples' assumptions, Jesus invites them to understand and embrace a paradigm shift rooted in grace, compassion, and the divine sovereignty of God. In doing so, He not only corrects their misinterpretation but also imparts a profound lesson about the mysteries of God's ways when someone encounters His grace.

Ultimately, Jesus' response serves as a starting point for deeper reflection and spiritual growth. This prompted the disciples and all who witnessed this encounter to embrace a more profound understanding of suffering, sin, and redemption. Yes, sin can cause sickness and afflictions such as blindness, but not in all cases.

The disciples obliviously did not know the man because they did not realize he had been blind since birth. Had they known, they wouldn't have questioned whether his blindness was a consequence of his own sins. Their understanding of discerning ailments and the nature of healing was limited, which would have hindered their ability to minister to him effectively. Rather than explicitly stating that sickness wasn't always tied to personal or generational sins, Jesus redirected their focus to the reason behind this man's blindness, a topic to be explored later in the book. The resolution to this question arises in Chapter Nine, where it becomes evident that some individuals experience illness and affliction to ultimately reveal the glory of God.

> *John 9:1-3 (ESV) As he passed by, he saw a man blind from birth. 2 And his disciples asked him, "Rabbi, who sinned, this man or his parents, that he was born blind?" 3 Jesus answered, "It was not that this man sinned, or his parents, but that the works of God might be displayed in him.*

What Can We Do?

What if the blindness was a result of personal sins? What can we do to change this? Let's keep the first things first.

Consider the possibility that the man's blindness could indeed be attributed to his personal sins. This raises a piercing question: What actions can we take to address such a scenario? Before delving into potential remedies, it's crucial to prioritize our approach by keeping the fundamental aspects in focus.

Acknowledging the prospect that personal sins might contribute to afflictions prompts us to reflect deeply on the nature of sin, its consequences, and the mechanisms of redemption. It calls for a profound examination of individual responsibility, the nature of suffering, and the transformative power of forgiveness and grace.

In contemplating how to address the potential connection between sin and affliction, it becomes evident that our initial focus must remain centered on foundational Biblical truths. We must first emphasize the importance of understanding and accepting the reality of sin, both in its individual and collective manifestations. This entails being convicted of God's righteousness and an awareness of sinfulness and the accountability God declares for transgressions within the individual.

Simultaneously, we must remember that Jesus always was moved with compassion. Therefore, we must uphold the principles of compassion, empathy, and support in our interactions with those who suffer, regardless of the perceived causes of their afflictions.

Moreover, we must engage in spiritual discernment to discern the underlying causes of suffering and discern the appropriate responses. This involves seeking guidance from God's Word, listening to the Holy Spirit, and spiritual mentors, to discern the answer to each situation and discern the most constructive course of action.

Ultimately, addressing the potential relationship between the individual's sin and their affliction necessitates a multifaceted approach that integrates theological reflection, spiritual discernment, and compassionate engagement. By keeping the foundational aspects of faith and compassion at the forefront of our endeavors, we can navigate the complexities of suffering within the bounds of the Father's wisdom, humility, and grace.

> *2 Timothy 2:24-26 (ESV) And the Lord's servant must not be quarrelsome but kind to everyone, able to teach, patiently enduring evil, 25 correcting his opponents with gentleness. God may perhaps grant them repentance leading to a knowledge of the truth, 26 and they may come to their senses and escape from the snare of the devil, after being captured by him to do his will.*

During the period when I was spiritually lost and adrift in darkness, I found myself sowing seeds of unrighteousness and nurturing destructive tendencies within my flesh. Recognizing that victory over the forces of evil that led to sickness requires a concerted effort. I have identified a threefold approach to follow: Repent, Root Out, and Replant.

REPENT (Turn Away From)

The initial step towards addressing afflictions caused by personal sins is to embark on a journey of repentance and transformation whereby one choses to stop the sin causing the sickness. This pivotal process begins with a sincere acknowledgment of our transgressions and a heartfelt commitment to forsake them.

Central to the Christian faith is coming to Christ for salvation involving a profound shift away from the patterns of sin and the allure of worldly pursuits. In embracing Christ, we signify our intention to turn away from the paths of darkness and embrace the path of God's righteousness.

> *Matthew 4:17 (ESV) From that time Jesus began to preach, saying, "Repent, for the kingdom of heaven is at hand."*
>
> *Luke 13:3 (ESV) No, I tell you; but unless you repent, you will all likewise perish.*
>
> *Luke 17:3 (ESV) Pay attention to yourselves! If your brother sins, rebuke him, and if he repents, forgive him,*
>
> *Acts 3:19 (ESV) Repent therefore, and turn back, that your sins may be blotted out,*

Repentance, fundamentally, entails a twofold transformation: a change of mind and a change of actions. It necessitates a profound shift in our attitudes, beliefs, and priorities, as well as a tangible alteration in our behaviors and choices. By embracing repentance, we signal our willingness to relinquish the hold of sin over our lives and embark on a journey of spiritual renewal and redemption found only in our Lord Jesus Christ and empowered by the indwelling of the Holy Spirit.

Essentially, the effectiveness of repentance in alleviating sickness, disease, and afflictions caused by personal sins hinges upon our commitment to wholeheartedly embrace this transformative process of a new life in Christ. Continual indulgence in sinful behaviors undermines the sincerity of true repentance and causes to continue the cycle of suffering and spiritual bondage.

Therefore, the imperative to repent and turn away from sin is not merely a theological abstraction but a Biblical and practical imperative with profound implications for our physical, emotional, and spiritual well-being. Healing and restoration are contingent upon our willingness to confront our sins, seek forgiveness, and pursue a path of righteousness and holiness.

For those who have yet to embark on this journey of repentance and reconciliation with Christ, the invitation remains open. It beckons us to humbly acknowledge our need for forgiveness, seek reconciliation with our heavenly Father, and embrace the transformative power of grace.

Ultimately, repentance calls for a radical reorientation of our entire being from the inside out. It is a spiritual transformation rooted in humility, contrition, and a steadfast commitment to walk in the light of our Lord's truth and righteousness. As we embrace the call to repentance and cultivate a mindset of renewal and transformation, we open ourselves to the boundless possibilities of healing, restoration, and spiritual wholeness found on in the redemptive work of our Lord Jesus Christ and the indwelling of the Holy Spirit.

> *2 Peter 3:9 (ESV) The Lord is not slow to fulfill his promise as some count slowness, but is patient toward you, not wishing that any should perish, but that all should reach repentance.*

ROOT OUT (Be Active And Violent Against Our Sins)

The next crucial step in addressing the impact of sin in our lives is to engage in the arduous task of tilling up the fallow ground or hardened soil ground of our hearts and choosing to resist the impulses and deeds of the flesh. Reflecting on my childhood, I vividly recall the annual ritual of my Granddaddy plowing his field in preparation for planting a garden. Each year, as he diligently turned over the soil, the only yield seemed to be an abundance of rocks. I would diligently collect these rocks in a cart, day after day, as my Granddaddy plowed, hauling them away to be dumped on the riverbank. Despite our efforts, the field never seemed entirely free of rocks, yet over time, their number dwindled, and their size diminished.

This process serves as a metaphor for the inner work we must undertake to confront the sins entrenched within our hearts, which perpetuate cycles of physical, mental, and emotional turmoil. It demands a resolute commitment to uprooting these destructive tendencies with unwavering determination. We need to become violent against them to root them out and haul them away.

> *Matthew 11:12 (ESV) From the days of John the Baptist until now the kingdom of heaven has suffered violence, and the violent take it by force.*

Sin operates within the framework of cause and effect—a fundamental principle governing the relationship between actions and their consequences. Just as every action triggers a reaction in the physical realm, the spiritual realm abides by the immutable law of cause and effect. The sinful disposition of our hearts serves as the cause, precipitating sinful actions and their subsequent repercussions (the effect).

> *Galatians 6:7-8 (ESV) Do not be deceived: God is not mocked, for whatever one sows, that will he also reap. 8 For the one who sows to his own flesh will from the flesh reap corruption, but the one who sows to the Spirit will from the Spirit reap eternal life.*

> *Jeremiah 4:3 (ESV) For thus says the LORD to the men of Judah and Jerusalem: "Break up your fallow ground, and sow not among thorns.*

To break free from this cycle of spiritual bondage, we must take proactive measures to eradicate the root causes of sin within our hearts. This necessitates a deliberate and often painful process of self-examination, repentance, and spiritual discipline. Just as my Granddaddy and I relentlessly pursued the removal of rocks from the field, we must adopt a similarly tenacious attitude towards confronting and overcoming the sins that entangle us.

Moreover, this endeavor demands a willingness to confront our innermost struggles with courage and conviction, refusing to succumb to the allure of complacency or resignation. Jesus came to destroy the works of the enemy. By actively engaging in the excavation of our hearts in the power of the Holy Spirit, we pave the way for transformation and renewal in Christ, breaking free from the shackles of sin and embracing the abundant life that awaits us.

> *1 John 3:5 (ESV) You know that he appeared in order to take away sins, and in him there is no sin.*
>
> *1 John 3:7-10 (ESV) Little children, let no one deceive you. Whoever practices righteousness is righteous, as he is righteous. 8 Whoever makes a practice of sinning is of the devil, for the devil has been sinning from the beginning. The reason the Son of God appeared was to destroy the works of the devil. 9 No one born of God makes a practice of sinning, for God's seed abides in him; and he cannot keep on sinning, because he has been born of God. 10 By this it is evident who are the children of God, and who are the children of the devil: whoever does not practice righteousness is not of God, nor is the one who does not love his brother.*

In essence, the journey towards spiritual wholeness and liberty requires a steadfast commitment to unearth the hidden recesses of our hearts, confronting the roots of sin with unwavering resolve. As we labor to cultivate fertile soil within our souls, we sow the seeds of righteousness from God's Word and reap the harvest of abundant life, liberated from the bondage of sin, and restored to the fullness of God's grace.

REPLANT (Sow A New Seed)

I started this healing process with this statement. During the period when I was spiritually lost and adrift in darkness, I found myself sowing seeds of unrighteousness and nurturing destructive tendencies within my flesh. Recognizing that victory over the forces of evil that led to sickness requires a concerted effort. I have identified a threefold approach to follow: Repent, Root Out, and Replant. The replanting stage is key to being healed and staying healed.

The first step we covered was repentance, which is essential. It involves acknowledging my sinful nature, the sins of the past, and committing to God's path of renewal and righteousness only found in Christ. By repenting, we confront our transgressions head-on, seeking forgiveness and restoration.

This stage often marks a critical juncture where individuals mistakenly equate confession with repentance. While confession involves acknowledging our sins and shortcomings, it does not inherently entail a proactive assault on the roots of sin or a deliberate choice to turn away from them.

Confession, in its essence, involves the courageous act of owning up to our failings and laying them bare before God and, perhaps, others. It means to agree with God concerning what He already sees and knows. It is an important step in the journey towards reconciliation and spiritual growth, as it fosters humility and accountability. However, the danger lies in stopping at confession without venturing further into the realm of repentance. True repentance demands more than mere acknowledgment; it requires a resolute determination to confront the roots of sin head-on and actively choose to redirect our lives towards righteousness. The word means to make and "about face."

The next phase we covered was rooting out, which demands a thorough excavation of the deep-seated sins that have taken root within our lives. This process is akin to uprooting weeds from a garden, requiring diligence and perseverance. It entails identifying and addressing the underlying causes of our sinful behaviors, dismantling them at their very core.

Repentance involves a deliberate and intentional turning away from sinful patterns and behaviors and a turning to God and His Word. It necessitates a radical reorientation of our hearts and minds, a steadfast commitment to forsake the allure of sin, and a wholehearted embrace of God's transformative grace.

Replanting signifies a transformative shift in our actions and attitudes. It involves replacing the barren soil of our hearts with the seeds of righteousness and grace from God's Word. While the intricacies of this replanting process will be explored further in Chapter 14, "Reaping What We Sow," it is imperative to begin cultivating this new crop in our lives and in the lives of those around us.

When replanting, establishing a habit of sowing righteousness is paramount. Just as a farmer carefully selects and nurtures seeds for a bountiful harvest, we must intentionally sow seeds of righteousness in our lives and in the lives of others. This deliberate cultivation fosters an environment conducive to spiritual growth and healing, yielding a harvest of blessings and transformation.

In essence, the journey towards victory over sickness and sin necessitates a proactive engagement with the principles of repentance, rooting out, and replanting. By embracing these transformative practices, we embark on a path of spiritual renewal and restoration, sowing seeds of righteousness that bear fruit in abundance.

Although it may initially sound reminiscent of self-help or relying solely on our efforts, the decision to actively confront sin and embrace righteousness is firmly rooted in the profound realities of faith in God and His Word. It is not merely a matter of human striving, but a conscious choice made possible by the transformative power of the cross, the presence of the indwelling Holy Spirit, and the purifying influence of God's Word.

At its core, this decision is a response to the redemptive work of Christ on the cross. Through His sacrificial death and resurrection, Jesus secured victory over sin and death, offering us the promise of forgiveness, reconciliation, and new life. It is within the framework of this profound truth that we find the strength and motivation to confront the grip of sin in our lives.

Furthermore, the indwelling presence of the Holy Spirit empowers and guides us in our journey of repentance and transformation. The Spirit serves as our advocate, counselor, and source of divine strength, enabling us to overcome the enticements of the flesh and walk in obedience to God's will. For those who walk in the Spirit will not fulfill the deeds of the flesh.

> *Galatians 5:16-17 (ESV) But I say, walk by the Spirit, and you will not gratify the desires of the flesh. 17 For the desires of the flesh are against the Spirit, and the desires of the Spirit are against the flesh, for these are opposed to each other, to keep you from doing the things you want to do.*

Moreover, the transformative power of God's Word plays a pivotal role in our spiritual renewal. Scripture serves as a lamp unto our feet and a light unto our path, illuminating the darkness of sin and offering timeless wisdom and guidance. Through the regular study, meditation, and application of God's Word, we are continually renewed and transformed, our minds and hearts conformed to the image of Christ.

> *Romans 12:1-2 (ESV) I appeal to you therefore, brothers, by the mercies of God, to present your bodies as a living sacrifice, holy and acceptable to God, which is your spiritual worship. 2 Do not be conformed to this world, but be transformed by the renewal of your mind, that by testing you may discern what is the will of God, what is good and acceptable and perfect.*

Far from being a product of human effort alone, the decision to confront sin and embrace righteousness is ultimately a response to the grace and mercy of God. It is a surrender to the transformative work of the cross, a reliance on the empowering presence of the Holy Spirit, and a submission to the purifying influence of God's Word.

Therefore, while it may seem like a mere exercise in self-help or works-based righteousness, the decision to confront sin and pursue holiness is firmly rooted in the profound realities of faith. It is a testament to the transformative power of God's grace at work within us, leading us ever closer to the fullness of life found in Christ.

> *Hosea 10:12-13 (ESV) Sow for yourselves righteousness; reap steadfast love; break up your fallow ground, for it is the time to seek the LORD, that he may come and rain righteousness upon you. 13 You have plowed iniquity; you have reaped injustice; you have eaten the fruit of lies. Because you have*

trusted in your own way and in the multitude of your warriors,

The Doctrine Of "Like Kind."

Before delving into further discussions about the origins of sickness, it's imperative to revisit the gravity with which we should regard our personal sins. Often, we underestimate the significance of our actions and fail to fully grasp the profound implications of transgressions against the Word and character of our Heavenly Father.

Each of our deeds, whether in thought, word, or action, holds weight in the spiritual realm, and they carry consequences that extend far beyond our immediate understanding. It's crucial to remember the timeless adage about sin: that it is not to be taken lightly.

The Doctrine Of "Like Kind" Says This.
- *You get WHAT you sow.*
- *You get MORE than you sow.*
- *You get it LATER than you sow.*

Sin, in its essence, represents a deviation from the divine standard set forth by God's Word and His character. It ruptures the harmonious relationship and fellowship between humanity and the Creator and introduces discord into the fabric of existence. Yet, in our daily lives, we often overlook the cumulative impact of our transgressions, dismissing them as insignificant or inconsequential.

However, the reality is that every sinful act carries with it a ripple effect, affecting not only our personal well-being but also the lives of those around us and the broader community. It erodes the moral fabric of society and

BE HEALED

tarnishes the witness of the Church, hindering our ability to reflect the transformative power of God's love and grace.

The choice to walk in the flesh rather than in the Spirit represents a fundamental decision that shapes our spiritual journey and relationship with our Heavenly Father. Scripture emphasizes that it is through faith—guided by the indwelling presence of the Holy Spirit—that we find favor in the eyes of God.

Walking in the flesh entails yielding to the desires and impulses of our human nature, which is prone to selfishness, pride, and worldly pursuits. This path leads us away from God's will and diminishes our capacity to experience the fullness of His love and grace. It fosters a mindset characterized by gratification of the senses and pursuit of temporal pleasures, often at the expense of spiritual growth and intimacy with God.

In contrast, walking in the Spirit requires a deliberate surrender to the leading and guidance of the Holy Spirit, who empowers us to live lives marked by faith, obedience, and righteousness. It involves aligning our thoughts, desires, and actions with the purposes of God, allowing His Spirit to transform us from within and conform us to the image of Christ.

Walking in faith is not merely a passive acknowledgment of God's existence, but an active response to His revealed truth and promises. It involves entrusting our lives entirely to His care and guidance, even when circumstances seem daunting or uncertain. It is through faith that we are justified before God, and it is by faith that we are able to please Him, as Hebrews 11:6 reminds us.

> *Hebrews 11:6 (ESV) And without faith it is impossible to please him, for whoever would draw near to God*

must believe that he exists and that he rewards those who seek him.

By walking in faith, we demonstrate our trust in God's sovereignty and goodness, regardless of the challenges or obstacles we may face. We anchor our hope in His unchanging character and unfailing love, knowing that He is faithful to fulfill His promises and lead us into abundant life.

In essence, walking in faith is a transformative journey that transcends the limitations of human understanding and opens the door to divine possibilities. It is a pathway of intimacy, obedience, and spiritual vitality, where our hearts are attuned to the heartbeat of God, and our lives bear witness to His transformative power.

Therefore, as we navigate the complexities of life, it behooves us to remain vigilant and mindful of our actions, recognizing the profound responsibility we bear as stewards of God's creation. Let us not trivialize the gravity of sin, but rather, let us strive for a life living by faith in our Lord Jesus Christ. Let us seek God's holiness and righteousness, while seeking forgiveness and redemption through the boundless mercy of our Heavenly Father.

In doing so, we honor the sacred trust bestowed upon us as children of God, and we embody the transformative power of His grace in a world desperately in need of healing and restoration. May we heed the admonition to take sin seriously, for in its acknowledgment lies the pathway to reconciliation, renewal, and abundant life in Christ. Let us remember this statement about sin.

BE HEALED

> Sin takes us further than we want to go.
> It costs us more than we want to pay.
> And it keeps us longer than we want to stay.

I'll state this again. The doctrine of ***"Like Kind"*** says this.
- *You get WHAT you sow.*
- *You get MORE than you sow.*
- *You get it LATER than you sow*

The principle of sowing and reaping underscores a fundamental truth about the consequences of our actions and choices. Just as farmers reap what they sow in their fields, so too do our deeds yield corresponding outcomes in our lives.

When we sow seeds of destruction through our actions, whether through unrighteousness, selfishness, or disobedience, we inevitably reap the fruit of that destruction. Our personal sins, like seeds planted in the soil of our lives, germinate, and grow into a harvest of physical, emotional, and mental turmoil.

> *James 1:13-15 (ESV) Let no one say when he is tempted, "I am being tempted by God," for God cannot be tempted with evil, and he himself tempts no one. 14 But each person is tempted when he is lured and enticed by his own desire. 15 Then desire when it has conceived gives birth to sin, and sin when it is fully grown brings forth death.*

The correlation between our actions and the consequences of sins are unmistakable. When we indulge in behaviors contrary to God's will and character, we set in motion a chain of events that culminate in adverse outcomes. The seeds of sin, once planted, take root and flourish, giving rise to a myriad of afflictions, ailments, and diseases that afflict our bodies, minds, and spirits.

The harvest of destruction that results from our personal sins is multifaceted and far-reaching. Physically, our bodies bear the brunt of the consequences, succumbing to illnesses, ailments, and infirmities that undermine our health and well-being. Emotionally, we experience the weight of guilt, shame, and regret, as the consequences of our actions take their toll on our innermost being. Mentally, our minds become ensnared in patterns of negativity, fear, and anxiety, robbing us of peace and clarity of thought.

Moreover, the ripple effects of our personal sins extend beyond the confines of our individual lives, impacting our relationships, communities, and spheres of influence. Our choices have the power to inflict pain and suffering on those around us, disrupting the harmony and unity that God intends for His creation. When we fail to walk in fellowship with the Holy Spirit and our Lord Jesus Christ we will fail at walking in a healthy and proper fellowship with our Christian brothers and sisters.

However, the principle of sowing and reaping is not confined to negative outcomes alone. Just as we reap destruction from seeds of sin, so too do we reap righteousness from seeds of obedience and faithfulness. When we sow seeds of righteousness—acts of kindness, compassion, and obedience to God's Word—we reap a harvest of blessing, joy, and abundance that enriches our lives and those around us.

Therefore, let us be mindful of the seeds we sow in the garden of our lives, knowing that each choice carries with it the potential for either blessing or destruction. May we strive to cultivate a heart that is fertile ground for righteousness, sowing seeds of obedience and faithfulness that yield a bountiful harvest of God's grace and goodness. In doing so, we align ourselves with the divine purpose and experience the abundant life that God desires for each of us.

> *Job 4:8-9 (ESV) As I have seen, those who plow iniquity and sow trouble reap the same. 9 By the breath of God they perish, and by the blast of his anger they are consumed.*
>
> *Proverbs 22:8 (ESV) Whoever sows injustice will reap calamity, and the rod of his fury will fail.*
>
> *Proverbs 1:22-33 (ESV) "How long, O simple ones, will you love being simple? How long will scoffers delight in their scoffing and fools hate knowledge? 23 If you turn at my reproof, behold, I will pour out my spirit to you; I will make my words known to you. 24 Because I have called and you refused to listen, have stretched out my hand and no one has heeded, 25 because you have ignored all my counsel and would have none of my reproof, 26 I also will laugh at your calamity; I will mock when terror strikes you, 27 when terror strikes you like a storm and your calamity comes like a whirlwind, when distress and anguish come upon you. 28 Then they will call upon me, but I will not answer; they will seek me diligently but will not find me. 29 Because they hated knowledge and did not choose the fear of the LORD, 30 would have none of my counsel and despised all my reproof, 31 therefore they shall eat the fruit of their way, and have their fill of their own devices. 32 For the simple are killed by their turning away, and the complacency of*

fools destroys them; 33 but whoever listens to me will dwell secure and will be at ease, without dread of disaster."

The Father Judges Our Deception And Rebellion

As we conclude this chapter, it's crucial to address the theme of the Father's judgment concerning our deception and rebellion. Throughout Scripture, we encounter instances where God discerns the intentions of the heart and evaluates the actions of individuals in light of His righteousness. We encounter teachings that emphasize God's discernment and response to human deceit and defiance.

Deception and rebellion represent a departure from God's truth and authority. When individuals engage in deceit or rebellion against God's will, they challenge His sovereignty and undermine the principles of righteousness and justice that govern His kingdom. Such actions not only betray a lack of trust in God's wisdom and guidance but also reflect a fundamental rejection of His divine authority.

The Father's judgment is not arbitrary or capricious but is rooted in His holiness and righteousness. He sees through the facade of deception and rebellion, discerning the motives behind our actions and holding us accountable for our choices. His judgment serves as a corrective measure, aiming to realign us with His purposes and restore harmony to our relationship with Him.

Moreover, the Father's judgment is characterized by His boundless love, mercy, and grace. Even in the face of human disobedience, He extends grace to those who humbly seek forgiveness and reconciliation. His judgment is tempered by compassion, as He seeks to draw us back into His loving embrace and lead us into paths of righteousness and restoration.

BE HEALED

Ultimately, the Father's judgment serves as a reminder of His sovereignty and authority over all creation. It underscores the importance of living in alignment with His will and obeying His commandments. While His judgment may provoke fear and awe, it also invites us into a deeper relationship with Him, submitting to the transformative power of His grace and mercy.

As we navigate the complexities of life, may we heed the Father's call to walk in submission, humility, truth, and obedience, knowing that His judgment is tempered by love and compassion. May we strive to cultivate hearts that are receptive to His guidance and open to His correction, trusting in His unfailing goodness and steadfast love. In doing so, we find refuge in His grace, even in the face of His discipline.

> *Proverbs 19:5 (ESV) A false witness will not go unpunished, and he who breathes out lies will not escape.*
>
> *Psalms 52:2-7 (ESV) Your tongue plots destruction, like a sharp razor, you worker of deceit. 3 You love evil more than good, and lying more than speaking what is right. Selah 4 You love all words that devour, O deceitful tongue. 5 But God will break you down forever; he will snatch and tear you from your tent; he will uproot you from the land of the living. Selah 6 The righteous shall see and fear, and shall laugh at him, saying, 7 "See the man who would not make God his refuge, but trusted in the abundance of his riches and sought refuge in his own destruction!"*

Chapter 4
SINS OF THE FOREFATHERS CAN CAUSE SICKNESS, ILLNESS, DISEASE AND DEATH

Exodus 20:5 (ESV) You shall not bow down to them or serve them, for I the LORD your God am a jealous God, visiting the iniquity of the fathers on the children to the third and the fourth generation of those who hate me,

The sins of our forefathers are also known as Generational sins or Generational sicknesses. Generational sins and sicknesses are patterns of sin or dysfunctions that pass down through family lines from one generation to the next. These patterns can manifest in various aspects of life, including physical health and emotional well-being.

An illustrative example of generational sins can be observed in the transmission of certain health conditions from one generation to another. For instance, diseases like heart disease or high blood pressure may recur across multiple generations within a family. Similarly, issues affecting the soul, such as generational depression, can also be inherited and perpetuated through familial lines.

In my own family history, the prevalence of generational sins became evident on my father's side. Among the nine children in his family, a consistent pattern emerged: all siblings suffered from breathing disorders and lung diseases, notably COPD. Additionally, they grappled with pervasive addictive tendencies that plagued their lives.

BE HEALED

The men in the family battled alcohol addiction, grappling with the destructive consequences of alcoholism. Meanwhile, the women struggled with food addiction, leading to obesity and related health challenges. These addictive behaviors became entrenched in family dynamics, casting a shadow over gatherings and interactions.

Amidst the challenges posed by generational sins, a common refrain emerged among family members. The three "Cs" of addictive behavior as listed below.

- *I didn't cause it.*
- *I can't cure it.*
- *I can't control it.*

"I didn't cause it" means they acknowledged the inheritance of these patterns from previous generations.

"I can't cure it" means they Recognized the complexities and difficulties inherent in overcoming addictive behaviors.

"I can't control it" means they came to terms with the limitations of personal agency in addressing these entrenched patterns. It could be a matter of not wanting to change. Therefore, the issue was a matter of the will.

The acknowledgment of generational sins serves as a sobering reminder of the pervasive impact of sin and dysfunction within families. It underscores the need for awareness, compassion, and proactive steps towards supernatural healing and restoration. By recognizing these patterns and seeking God's deliverance, individuals and families can break free from the cycle of generational sins, fostering healing and wholeness for future generations.

How Did This Affect Me?

The phrase "you can't pick the family you came from" often evokes a sense of humor in me, as I reflect on my own familial lineage. I love them, but I find myself belonging to a lineage that seems to be characterized by a long history of what some might label as "bad genes."

This sentiment carries layers of complexity and irony. While we cannot choose the genetic inheritance or family background we are born into, the realities of our lineage often shape our experiences and perceptions in profound ways. In my case, the narrative of my family's genetic predispositions adds a unique dimension to my understanding of self and identity and answered the why's of some of my past behavioral patterns.

The impact of growing up amidst generational sins and familial dysfunction has left a profound imprint on my life, shaping my experiences, and influencing my choices in significant ways. While some may attribute these patterns to learned behavior stemming from my upbringing, I view them through a spiritual and Biblical lens, recognizing the inherent truth in the scriptural principle that the sins of the forefathers can be visited upon the children.

In grappling with the implications of my familial lineage, I find myself navigating a terrain marked by both challenges and opportunities. While there may be spiritual and genetic inheritances that predispose me to certain vulnerabilities or tendencies, there is also room for how I respond to and deal with these predispositions.

Moreover, the recognition of "bad genes" prompts deeper reflections on the broader concept of spiritual strongholds in terms of values, beliefs, and traditions passed down through generations. It caused me to investigate the paths that have shaped my family's history and consider how they continue to influence my own journey of walking with my heavenly Father in spiritual growth.

Ultimately, while I may have emerged from a lineage characterized by what some might perceive as "bad genes," I refuse to be defined by this. Instead, I embrace my heritage as integral to my earthly identity. However, my real identity is now defined as a child of God and belonging to the kingdom of heaven.

I would like to share my personal walk-through life. During my formative years as a young adult, before embracing Christ, I found myself ensnared in the grip of addiction, grappling with the destructive allure of alcohol and drugs. The echoes of addiction reverberated through my family history, mirroring the struggles of my father, aunts, and uncles who battled similar demons. It became evident to me that the seeds of addiction had been sown generations ago, manifesting as a cyclical pattern that permeated our familial landscape.

Moreover, the physical toll of generational sins became apparent as I witnessed the prevalence of heart (CHF) and lung disease, particularly COPD, among myself and my siblings. This affliction, passed down through familial lines, served as a stark reminder of the interconnectedness between physical health and spiritual inheritance.

While the worldly environmental perspective may offer explanations rooted in learned behavior and predisposition, I find solace in the spiritual truths embedded within Scripture. The acknowledgment of generational sins invites us to confront the complexities of our genetic legacies, recognizing the profound implications they hold for our spiritual, mental, emotional, and physical well-being.

For me, the journey towards healing and restoration began with a supernatural transformative encounter with the Lord Jesus Christ. Through His redemptive grace, I was saved and found freedom from the shackles of addiction and discovered a renewed sense of purpose and identity. As I continue to navigate the complexities of life, I am reminded of the transformative power of God's love and mercy, which transcends the limitations of generational curses and offers the promise of redemption and restoration for all who turn to Him in faith. Jesus came to free us from the power of the enemy and the strongholds in our lives.

> *1 John 3:8 (ESV) Whoever makes a practice of sinning is of the devil, for the devil has been sinning from the beginning. The reason the Son of God appeared was to destroy the works of the devil.*

In embracing the spiritual healing found in the cleansing blood of our Lord Jesus Christ, I am empowered to break free from the chains of generational bondage, charting a new course characterized by healing, wholeness, and divine purpose. Through Christ, I am reminded that while the sins of the forefathers may cast a shadow over my past, His grace illuminates the path towards a future marked by hope, redemption, and abundant life.

> *Philippians 3:12-14 (ESV) Not that I have already obtained this or am already perfect, but I press on to make it my own, because Christ Jesus has made me his own. 13 Brothers, I do not consider that I have made it my own. But one thing I do: forgetting what lies behind and straining forward to what lies ahead, 14 I press on toward the goal for the prize of the upward call of God in Christ Jesus.*

BE HEALED

Hebrews 12:1-2 (ESV) Therefore, since we are surrounded by so great a cloud of witnesses, let us also lay aside every weight, and sin which clings so closely, and let us run with endurance the race that is set before us, 2 looking to Jesus, the founder and perfecter of our faith, who for the joy that was set before him endured the cross, despising the shame, and is seated at the right hand of the throne of God.

I could have adopted the three "C's" approach to the challenges I encountered. I could have taken the easy way out and resigned myself to labeling the ailments, sicknesses, diseases, afflictions, and addictions with the mantra: "I didn't *cause* them, I can't *cure* them, and I can't *control* them." This approach might have led me to embrace the "Que Sera, Sera" mentality—an acceptance that "Whatever will be, will be." This philosophy suggests that the future is uncertain, and I am resigned to accepting whatever fate comes my way, making the best of the cards I've been dealt. However, such a perspective raises a critical question: Where does God, His Word, grace, power, and salvation fit into this form of humanistic thinking?

Let's delve into several piercing Biblical examples illustrating the profound implications of the sins of the fathers being visited upon the children. One such case is that of Eli, the Priest, whose narrative in 1 Samuel chapters 2-4, serves as a sobering reminder of the far-reaching consequences of parental negligence and spiritual apathy.

Eli, entrusted with the sacred duty of priesthood, found himself grappling with profound failures in his role as both a father and a spiritual leader. Despite his position of authority, Eli failed to exercise proper discipline over his sons, Hophni and Phinehas, allowing them to indulge in flagrant disobedience and moral corruption. Moreover, Eli's spiritual discernment waned over time, leading to a lamentable loss of sensitivity to the presence and will of the Lord.

The repercussions of Eli's shortcomings reverberated throughout the community, as his sons descended into moral depravity and earned a notorious reputation for their ungodly behavior. Their actions cast a shadow over the sanctity of the priesthood and undermined the spiritual integrity of the entire nation. The outrageousness of their transgressions culminated in a series of tragic events. We read about the untimely deaths of Hophni and Phinehas in battle, the demise of Eli himself upon hearing the devastating news, and the subsequent capture of the Ark of the Covenant by the Philistines.

Eli's story serves as a cautionary tale, highlighting the profound impact of parental influence and the weight of spiritual responsibility entrusted to those in positions of authority. His failure to confront and correct the moral decay within his own household resulted in catastrophic consequences, ultimately leading to the loss of lives and the desecration of the sacred and holy things dedicated to God by God.

Eli's story underscores the interconnectedness between individual accountability and the well-being of the city and nation. His reluctance to confront sin within his family not only compromised his own spiritual standing but also had far-reaching implications for the entire nation. It serves as a intense and painful reminder of the sobering reality that our actions, as parents and leaders, carry profound implications for future generations.

In reflecting on Eli's tragic life, we are compelled to examine our own lives and relationships, recognizing the weight of our choices and the far-reaching impact of our actions. May we heed the lessons embedded within Scripture, cultivating hearts of humility, discernment, and obedience to God's will, as we strive to honor Him in all aspects of our lives.

When considering the legacies passed down to us from our ancestors or the seeds we sowed in our lives prior to our salvation experience, it becomes imperative to acknowledge their potential hold over us and their implications for future generations. Whether it be generational patterns of behavior, cultural traditions, or personal struggles, these inherited or cultivated influences have the power to shape our identities and impact the lives of those who come after us.

In recognizing the significance of these legacies, we are called to a profound sense of responsibility—one that extends beyond our own individual lives to encompass the well-being and spiritual health of our children and descendants. Just as we have inherited certain traits or tendencies from our forebears, so too do we possess the capacity to pass down both blessings and burdens to future generations. We do not want to pass generational sins and strongholds to our children or grandchildren.

Therefore, it behooves us to undertake a deliberate and intentional process of discernment and deliverance—a journey aimed at breaking the hold of negative patterns or influences that threaten to perpetuate cycles of dysfunction or spiritual bondage. This entails a commitment to self-examination, prayer, fasting, and the diligent pursuit of healing and restoration.

Central to this process is the recognition that our salvation experience marks a pivotal moment of transition—a divine opportunity to break free from the chains of our past and embrace the fullness of God's redemptive grace. We must appropriate all that Christ did for us on the cross.

Through the power of Christ's sacrifice and the indwelling presence of the Holy Spirit, we are empowered to confront and overcome the generational strongholds and personal struggles that seek to ensnare us.

In seeking to break the hold of these inherited or cultivated influences, we are guided by the transformative truths of Scripture and the abiding presence of God's Spirit within us. Through prayer, repentance, and obedience to God's Word, we position ourselves to experience the liberating power of His grace and the restoration of His purposes for our lives. Chains of strongholds will be broken from us and the influential cycle of generational sins passed to our children until the fourth generation cancelled.

As we embark on this journey of spiritual renewal in Christ, we do so not only for our own sake but also for the sake of future generations. By breaking the cycle of spiritual bondage and embracing the fullness of God's redemptive work in our lives, we pave the way for a legacy of faith, wholeness, and blessing to be passed down to our children and their descendants.

In this way, our pursuit of spiritual freedom becomes not only a personal endeavor but also a sacred responsibility—a commitment to honor God and bless future generations by breaking the chains of bondage and embracing the abundant life that He offers to all who call upon His name.

> *Psalms 78:4 (ESV) We will not hide them from their children, but tell to the coming generation the glorious deeds of the LORD, and his might, and the wonders that he has done.*

Psalms 78:6-8 (ESV) that the next generation might know them, the children yet unborn, and arise and tell them to their children, 7 so that they should set their hope in God and not forget the works of God, but keep his commandments; 8 and that they should not be like their fathers, a stubborn and rebellious generation, a generation whose heart was not steadfast, whose spirit was not faithful to God.

1 Samuel 2:17 (ESV) Thus the sin of the young men was very great in the sight of the LORD, for the men treated the offering of the LORD with contempt.

1 Samuel 2:22-25 (ESV) Now Eli was very old, and he kept hearing all that his sons were doing to all Israel, and how they lay with the women who were serving at the entrance to the tent of meeting. 23 And he said to them, "Why do you do such things? For I hear of your evil dealings from all these people. 24 No, my sons; it is no good report that I hear the people of the LORD spreading abroad. 25 If someone sins against a man, God will mediate for him, but if someone sins against the LORD, who can intercede for him?" But they would not listen to the voice of their father, for it was the will of the LORD to put them to death.

1 Samuel 3:11-14 (ESV) Then the LORD said to Samuel, "Behold, I am about to do a thing in Israel at which the two ears of everyone who hears it will tingle. 12 On that day I will fulfill against Eli all that I have spoken concerning his house, from beginning to end. 13 And I declare to him that I am about to punish his house forever, for the iniquity that he knew, because his sons were blaspheming God, and he did not restrain them. 14 Therefore I swear to the house of Eli that the iniquity of Eli's house shall not be atoned for by sacrifice or offering forever."

1 Samuel 4:4 (ESV) So the people sent to Shiloh and brought from there the ark of the covenant of the LORD of hosts, who is enthroned on the cherubim. And the two sons of Eli, Hophni and Phinehas, were there with the ark of the covenant of God.

1 Samuel 4:10-11 (ESV) So the Philistines fought, and Israel was defeated, and they fled, every man to his home. And there was a very great slaughter, for thirty thousand foot soldiers of Israel fell. 11 And the ark of God was captured, and the two sons of Eli, Hophni and Phinehas, died.

1 Samuel 4:16-18 (ESV) And the man said to Eli, "I am he who has come from the battle; I fled from the battle today." And he said, "How did it go, my son?" 17 He who brought the news answered and said, "Israel has fled before the Philistines, and there has also been a great defeat among the people. Your two sons also, Hophni and Phinehas, are dead, and the ark of God has been captured." 18 As soon as he mentioned the ark of God, Eli fell over backward from his seat by the side of the gate, and his neck was broken and he died, for the man was old and heavy. He had judged Israel forty years.

The People In Jesus' Day Understood The Consequences Of Generational Sins

The context of Jesus' time illuminates a stark awareness among the people regarding the weight of generational sins and their enduring consequences. As Jesus stood before a mock court, Pontius Pilate, the Roman governor, found himself entangled in a moment of profound moral dilemma. He posed a question to the gathered crowd, seeking their judgment on the fate of Jesus: "What then shall I do with Jesus who is called Christ?"

The response from the assembled throng, goaded on by the religious leaders, echoed with chilling clarity: "Let Him be crucified!" The collective outcry of condemnation reverberated through the air, as the people, swept up in a wave of fervent emotion and religious fervor, demanded the crucifixion of the innocent Son of God.

In a pathetic gesture of symbolic absolution, Pilate sought to distance himself from the grave injustice unfolding before him. He ceremoniously washed his hands, a gesture intended to signify his avowed innocence in the matter. "I am innocent of the blood of this just person," he declared, seeking to absolve himself of responsibility for the impending crucifixion.

Yet, amidst the tumult and chaos of that fateful moment, a haunting proclamation emerged—one that captured the weight of generational sins and their enduring impact on the people of Israel. In Matthew 27:25, we hear the chilling declaration uttered by the crowd: "His blood be on us and on our children."

This solemn utterance carries profound implications, echoing the somber reality of the consequences of generational sins visited upon successive generations. The people, in their fervent zeal and misguided allegiance to tradition, unwittingly invoked a curse upon themselves and their descendants—a curse that would reverberate through the annals of history, shaping the destiny of the nation and its people.

In their rejection of the Messiah, the people of Israel bore witness to the tragic consequences of generational sin and spiritual blindness. Their refusal to acknowledge Jesus as the long-awaited Savior paved the way for a cataclysmic chain of events—the crucifixion of the innocent Lamb of God, the atoning sacrifice for the sins of humanity, and the eventual dispersion of the Jewish nation.

In the unfolding drama of Jesus' crucifixion, we witness the collision of divine sovereignty and human weakness, as the consequences of generational sins intersect with the unfolding plan of redemption. It serves as a sober reminder of the enduring significance of our choices and the profound implications of generational legacies, underscoring the imperative of repentance, reconciliation, and redemption in the face of sin's devastating consequences.

> *Matthew 27:22-25 (ESV) Pilate said to them, "Then what shall I do with Jesus who is called Christ?" They all said, "Let him be crucified!" 23 And he said, "Why? What evil has he done?" But they shouted all the more, "Let him be crucified!" 24 So when Pilate saw that he was gaining nothing, but rather that a riot was beginning, he took water and washed his hands before the crowd, saying, "I am innocent of this man's blood; see to it yourselves." 25 And all the people answered, "His blood be on us and on our children!"*

Now, let us reflect on the repercussions of the statement found in Matthew 27:25 for the Jewish people throughout the span of the last nineteen hundred years.

What Can We Do?

To break the generational sins of our forefathers, a deliberate course of action is required—one that entails repentance and renunciation of the sins and sicknesses that have plagued our familial lineage. Central to this process is the recognition of the transformative power of the Blood of the Lord Jesus Christ and His sacrificial work on the cross — a covenant that transcends the limitations of our natural birth.

When Jesus willingly surrendered Himself to the agony of the cross, He did so with a divine purpose: to break the chains of bondage and to liberate humanity from the curses that have plagued us for generations. His atoning sacrifice represents a higher covenant — one that supersedes the constraints of our earthly lineage and offers a pathway to spiritual freedom and renewal.

However, the power and authority of Christ's redemptive work hinges upon our response of faith and appropriation. Through faith, we have the privilege of accessing the victory secured for us by Jesus Christ — a victory that holds the power to break the generational curses that have ensnared us and our ancestors.

Personal confession and repentance serve as the catalyst for this transformative process, as we acknowledge the weight of our ancestral sins and their implications for our lives. By renouncing the patterns of disobedience and spiritual bondage that have characterized our family lineage, we position ourselves to receive the fullness of God's grace and restoration.

Moreover, our journey towards breaking generational curses is marked by a steadfast commitment to prayer, obedience, and spiritual warfare. Armed with the truth of God's Word and the authority bestowed upon us as children of God, we engage in spiritual warfare, demolishing strongholds and declaring victory over the forces of darkness that seek to oppress us.

> *2 Corinthians 10:3-6 (ESV) For though we walk in the flesh, we are not waging war according to the flesh. 4 For the weapons of our warfare are not of the flesh but have divine power to destroy strongholds. 5 We destroy arguments and every lofty opinion raised against the knowledge of God, and take every thought captive to obey Christ, 6 being ready to punish every disobedience, when your obedience is complete.*

> *Ephesians 6:11-13 (ESV) Put on the whole armor of God, that you may be able to stand against the schemes of the devil. 12 For we do not wrestle against flesh and blood, but against the rulers, against the authorities, against the cosmic powers over this present darkness, against the spiritual forces of evil in the heavenly places. 13 Therefore take up the whole armor of God, that you may be able to withstand in the evil day, and having done all, to stand firm.*

In the face of daunting challenges and entrenched patterns of sin, we cling to the promise of God's faithfulness and the supernatural transformative power of His Spirit. Through unwavering faith and dependence on His grace, we walk in the assurance of victory, confident that He who has begun a good work in us will bring it to completion.

As we embark on this journey of spiritual renewal and liberation, may we be steadfast in our resolve, unwavering in our faith, and unyielding in our pursuit of righteousness. In the name of Jesus Christ, may the generational curses that have plagued us be broken, and may we experience the fullness of His freedom and abundant life.

> *Galatians 3:13-14 (ESV) Christ redeemed us from the curse of the law by becoming a curse for us—for it is*

written, "Cursed is everyone who is hanged on a tree"— 14 so that in Christ Jesus the blessing of Abraham might come to the Gentiles, so that we might receive the promised Spirit through faith.

Chapter 5
WORD CURSES CAN CAUSE SICKNESS, ILLNESS, DISEASE, AND DEATH

Word curses are also known as "self-fulfilled prophecies" wield a profound influence on our physical and emotional health, capable of precipitating sickness, disease, and even death. Consider the scenario where individuals grow up subjected to a constant barrage of demeaning messages, repeatedly told that they are stupid or worthless. Over time, these insidious word curses embed themselves deeply within the psyche, shaping beliefs and behaviors in ways that validate and perpetuate the negative projections cast upon them.

The insidious nature of word curses lies in their ability to infiltrate the subconscious mind, shaping perceptions and self-image in subtle yet pervasive ways. It's important to acknowledge that while word curses can significantly impact us, it doesn't negate the reality that demonic forces may exploit these openings to oppress us further.

As individuals internalize these negative messages, they unwittingly set in motion a self-fulfilling prophecy, unwittingly aligning their thoughts, words, and actions with the limiting beliefs imposed upon them.

These word curses often manifest as self-imposed limitations, enclosed in statements like "I can't do this" or "I'm not smart enough for that." By giving voice to these self-limiting beliefs, individuals inadvertently invite physical, mental, and emotional ailments into their lives, perpetuating a cycle of negativity and self-sabotage.

BE HEALED

Indeed, the power of words to shape our reality cannot be overstated. Proverbs 18:21 attests to this timeless truth: "Death and life are in the power of the tongue." The words we speak have the potential to breathe life and blessings into our circumstances or usher in destruction and curses.

> *Proverbs 18:19-21 (ESV) A brother offended is more unyielding than a strong city, and quarreling is like the bars of a castle. 20 From the fruit of a man's mouth his stomach is satisfied; he is satisfied by the yield of his lips. 21* **Death and life are in the power of the tongue**, *and those who love it will eat its fruits.*

Medical professionals increasingly recognize the profound impact of thoughts, emotions, and confessions on physical health and well-being. Studies reveal that patients in hospital settings can experience remarkable improvements in their condition simply by changing their mindset and adopting a more positive and spiritual outlook.

In light of these revelations, it becomes imperative to exercise discernment and intentionality in our speech, recognizing the immense power vested in the spoken word. The adage "It is better to keep your mouth shut and let people think you are a fool than to open it and remove all doubt" underscores the wisdom of exercising restraint and thoughtfulness in our communication.

As we navigate the complexity of life, may we be mindful of the words we speak, recognizing their capacity to shape our reality and influence our well-being. Let us choose words from the kingdom of heaven that edify, uplift, and inspire. Let's speak healing and empowerment into our lives and the lives of those around us.

Proverbs 15:4 (ESV) A gentle tongue is a tree of life, but perverseness in it breaks the spirit.

Proverbs 15:28 (ESV) The heart of the righteous ponders how to answer, but the mouth of the wicked pours out evil things.

*Proverbs 13:3 (ESV) Whoever guards his mouth preserves his life; he who **opens wide his lips comes to ruin**.*

*Proverbs 12:13 (ESV) An evil man is **ensnared by the transgression of his lips,** but the righteous escapes from trouble.*

Blessings And Curses Flow From The Same Well

*James 3:5-12 (ESV) So also the tongue is a small member, yet it boasts of great things. How great a forest is set ablaze by such a small fire! 6 And the tongue is a fire, a world of unrighteousness. The tongue is set among our members, staining the whole body, setting on fire the entire course of life, and set on fire by hell. 7 For every kind of beast and bird, of reptile and sea creature, can be tamed and has been tamed by mankind, 8 but no human being can tame the tongue. It is a restless evil, full of deadly poison. 9 With it we bless our Lord and Father, and with it we curse people who are made in the likeness of God. 10 **From the same mouth come blessing and cursing.** My brothers, these things ought not to be so. 11 Does a spring pour forth from the same opening both fresh and salt water? 12 Can a fig tree, my brothers, bear olives, or a grapevine produce figs? Neither can a salt pond yield fresh water.*

BE HEALED

In James 3:5-12, we encounter a profound truth regarding the dual nature of blessings and curses—they spring forth from the same wellspring, poised to shape the course of our lives and interactions with others.

The passage begins by likening the tongue to a small but potent flame that possesses the capacity to ignite vast expanses of forest. In much the same way, the tongue, though seemingly inconsequential in size, wields immense power to influence and shape our reality. It serves as the conduit through which blessings and curses flow forth, leaving a permanent imprint on the world around us.

James draws attention to the inherent contradiction present within the tongue—a vessel capable of both blessing and cursing. He underscores the absurdity of this paradox, likening it to a fountain that spews forth both fresh water and bitter water. Such mismatched examples highlight the pivotal role our words play in shaping the direction of our lives and relationships.

The apostle further emphasizes the impossibility of reconciling blessings and curses, likening them to fig trees that cannot bear olives or grapevines that cannot produce figs. He underscores the inherent inconsistency of a tongue that professes to bless God while simultaneously cursing those made in His image.

James compellingly argues that such contradiction reveals a deeper issue—the condition of the heart. Just as a fountain cannot simultaneously produce fresh water and bitter water, so too does the tongue betray the true state of one's innermost being. He challenges believers to confront the root cause of their speech patterns, urging them to cultivate hearts characterized by purity, humility, and reverence for God. If we are to speak the truth, we are to do so in the love of God.

> *Ephesians 4:14-16 (ESV) so that we may no longer be children, tossed to and fro by the waves and carried about by every wind of doctrine, by human cunning, by craftiness in deceitful schemes. 15 Rather, speaking the truth in love, we are to grow up in every way into him who is the head, into Christ, 16 from whom the whole body, joined and held together by every joint with which it is equipped, when each part is working properly, makes the body grow so that it builds itself up in love.*

Moreover, James underscores the enduring impact of our words, likening them to ships that navigate the vast expanse of the sea. Just as a small rudder steers a mighty vessel, so too do our words chart the course of our lives, shaping destinies and leaving a lasting legacy in their wake.

Considering this sobering truth, James exhorts believers to exercise vigilance and discernment in their speech, recognizing the immense power vested in the tongue. He urges them to cultivate lives characterized by wisdom, humility, and integrity, seeking to align their words with the truth of God's Word.

Ultimately, James invites believers to embrace the profound responsibility entrusted to them—to steward the gift of speech in a manner that glorifies God, edifies others, and reflects the transformative power of His love and grace. In doing so, they participate in the redemptive work of God, giving blessings that flow forth from the same wellspring as curses, and ushering in a kingdom marked by righteousness, peace, and joy in the Holy Spirit.

BE HEALED

> *Romans 14:17 (ESV) For the kingdom of God is not a matter of eating and drinking but of righteousness and peace and joy in the Holy Spirit.*

Foolish Lips

During my teenage years, my father cautioned me about the potential consequences of my outspoken nature. He likened my propensity for verbal confrontation to a battleship that could capsize my small vessel of diplomacy. The actual way my dad communicated it was that one day my battleship mouth would sink my dinky boat bottom.

His words proved prophetic. As a young man, I found myself entangled in numerous conflicts fueled by the words that escaped my lips, often more than I could effectively manage or resolve.

> *Proverbs 18:6-7 (ESV)* **<u>A fool's lips walk into a fight, and his mouth invites a beating.</u>** *7 A fool's mouth is his ruin, and his lips are a snare to his soul.*

Life and Death Are In The Tongue

> *Proverbs 18:19-21 (ESV) A brother offended is more unyielding than a strong city, and quarreling is like the bars of a castle. 20 From the fruit of a man's mouth his stomach is satisfied; he is satisfied by the yield of his lips. 21* **<u>Death and life are in the power of the tongue</u>**, *and those who love it will eat its fruits.*

Proverbs 18:19-21 starts with what happens when the ministry of offense occurs between relationships. Verse 19 highlights the power of offense and quarreling. It suggests that when any close relationship is offended, the rift created is often harder to mend than even the defenses of a fortified city. We see that quarreling, or engaging in prolonged disputes, can create barriers and divisions as strong as the bars of a castle's gate. The verse linked with verses 20 and 21 underscores the importance of avoiding unnecessary conflict and being mindful of how our actions may affect others, especially our words.

In verse 20 we see the impact of one's words on their own life. The words we speak have consequences, just like the fruit of a tree sustains us physically, the words we speak can either bring satisfaction or dissatisfaction to our lives. In other words, our speech has the power to affect our own well-being and fulfillment. When linked to verse 19, we see the implication that our words can carry the consequences of broken relationships.

Verse 21 expresses the profound influence of speech. It acknowledges that the tongue, or our words, hold immense power. The words from our lips can bring either death or life. Words have the potential to harm or heal, or to destroy or build up. The phrase "those who love it will eat its fruits" implies that those who use their words will experience the consequences, whether positive or negative.

Our Words Reveal Our Hearts

> Matthew 12:33-37 (ESV) "Either make the tree good and its fruit good, or make the tree bad and its fruit bad, **for the tree is known by its fruit.** 34 You brood of vipers! **How can you speak good, when you are evil? For out of the abundance of the heart the mouth speaks.** 35 The good person out of his good treasure brings forth good, and the evil person out of his evil treasure brings forth evil. 36 I tell you, on the day of judgment **people will give account for every**

BE HEALED

careless word they speak, 37 **for by your words you will be justified, and by your words you will be condemned.**"

Matthew 12:33-37 begins with the metaphor of a tree and its fruit to illustrate a principle about character and actions. Just as a good tree produces good fruit and a bad tree produces bad fruit, our actions and words are indicative of our inner character. In other words, the quality of our speech and actions reflects the condition of our heart.

In verse 34 our Lord Jesus Christ addresses the Pharisees, who were known for their outward piety but lacked genuine salvation or goodness in their hearts. Jesus accuses them of being like a brood of vipers, accusing them of their hypocrisy and wickedness. He emphasizes that the words they speak reveal the true state of their hearts. This is a law we need to keep in mind in self-examination and evaluation of those claiming to know Christ. Whatever fills the heart will eventually overflow through speech and actions.

Verse 35 is basically a summary of verses 33-34. It reiterates the principle that what is in the heart influences the words and actions that come forth. A person who is genuinely born again and walking with God will naturally produce good words and deeds, while someone who is evil will produce evil words and deeds.

Matthew 12: 36-37 are sobering verses which underscore the seriousness of our words and actions. Jesus emphasizes that we will be held accountable for every word we speak, including those spoken carelessly or thoughtlessly. Our words will ultimately be used as evidence either for or against us on the day of judgment. Think about this. Our words are a mirror or reflection of our character and will contribute as a witness against us as to whether we are justified or condemned.

While our salvation is not determined by the words we speak, the Bible emphasizes that our words reveal the condition of our hearts and serve as evidence of our faith and relationship with God. Our words, therefore, carry profound significance in the context of salvation.

It's crucial to understand that salvation is a matter of the heart and is ultimately a gift from God, granted through faith in Jesus Christ. Our words do not save us; rather, it is the grace of God and our response of faith that bring about salvation.

However, the words we speak are indicative of the state of our hearts and the authenticity of our faith. Just as Jesus taught in Matthew 12:33-37, the fruit of a tree reflects its nature, as our words reflect the condition of our hearts. If our hearts are transformed by the saving grace of Jesus Christ, our words will naturally reflect that transformation. We will speak words of love, kindness, truth, and grace, bearing witness to the work of God within us.

Conversely, if our hearts remain unchanged and devoid of genuine faith, our words may betray that emptiness and bare witness against us. Words of malice, deceit, hatred, and unbelief may flow from a heart that has not experienced the transformative power of God's love.

Therefore, while our words themselves do not determine our salvation, they serve as a testimony of our relationship with God. On the day of judgment, our words will be brought forth as evidence, either affirming our faith and salvation or standing as a witness against us.

In essence, our words reveal whether we possess salvation or not, and they stand as a testimony for or against us. They are not the means of salvation but rather the evidence of a transformed life in Christ. As followers of Jesus, we are called to let our words be seasoned with grace, reflecting the love and truth of our Savior, and bearing witness to the salvation that we have received by faith.

In summary, Matthew 12:33-37 teaches us that our words reveal the condition of our hearts and that we will be judged based on the fruit of our words and actions. It underscores the importance of cultivating a heart that is aligned with goodness and righteousness, which will naturally lead to words and actions that honor God. The foundational principle expressed here is echoed in Matthew 15:10-11 and 15:17-20 as well.

> *Matthew 15:10-11 (ESV) And he called the people to him and said to them, "Hear and understand: 11 it is not what goes into the mouth that defiles a person, but* **what comes out of the mouth; this defiles a person**.*"*

> *Matthew 15:17-20 (ESV) Do you not see that whatever goes into the mouth passes into the stomach and is expelled? 18* **But what comes out of the mouth proceeds from the heart, and this defiles a person.** *19 For out of the heart come evil thoughts, murder, adultery, sexual immorality, theft, false witness, slander. 20 These are what defile a person. But to eat with unwashed hands does not defile anyone."*

In this chapter, we've explored a significant concept: the potential for ailments, sicknesses, afflictions, and diseases to emerge through the expression of word curses spoken forth from the heart. We've observed how the words we speak can have tangible effects on our well-being and the well-being of others with the power of life and blessings or death and curses.

What Can We Do?

In our daily lives, it's common for us to speak without fully considering the impact of our words. Often, we inadvertently utter word curses over ourselves and others without even realizing it. As believers, we may sometimes dismiss the significance of our words, viewing teachings on this matter as excessive or overly zealous. However, when we examine the Scriptures, we find considerable attention given to the power of our speech. Perhaps, then, it's worth exercising greater discernment regarding what we allow to escape our lips.

Consider the seemingly innocent phrases we casually utter, believing them to be harmless chatter. For instance, when we sneeze or cough, how often do we jokingly say, "I think I'm trying to catch a cold"? It's absurd to think that anyone would intentionally seek to catch a cold, yet we speak these words without much thought. What if, instead, we trained ourselves to speak words of faith and affirmation? This isn't merely about engaging in positive thinking; it's about embracing the power of faith and trust in God and His Word.

It's essential to recognize that the words we speak reflect what resides in our hearts—the depth of our beliefs and faith. Our actions and the words that flow from our lips reveal the true nature of our convictions. Therefore, by consciously choosing to align our speech with faith and trust in God, we not only uplift ourselves but also contribute to the manifestation of His promises in our lives.

BE HEALED

In essence, by paying closer attention to the words we speak and infusing them with faith and belief in God's goodness and provision, we can harness the transformative power of our speech. This isn't about mere positive confession; it's about embracing a deeper understanding of faith in God's Word and allowing the character of the Father to permeate every aspect of our lives, including the words we utter.

In Psalm 141:3-4, we find King David expressing profound insight into the significance of words. David's prayer reflects a deep awareness of the potential harm that can result from the words we speak. In his plea to God, David humbly requests divine intervention in the form of a guard over his mouth.

> *Psalms 141:3-4 (ESV)* **Set a guard, O LORD, over my mouth**; *keep watch over the door of my lips! 4 Do not let my heart incline to any evil, to busy myself with wicked deeds in company with men who work iniquity, and let me not eat of their delicacies!*

David's prayer is an acknowledgment of the power and influence of speech. He recognizes the importance of exercising caution and restraint in what he says, understanding that words have the ability to bring either life or destruction. By petitioning God to set a guard over his mouth, David demonstrates a heartfelt desire to speak words that honor God and build up others.

This prayer reveals David's awareness of his own vulnerability to temptation and sin, particularly in the realm of speech. He understands that without the Father's intervention and guidance, he is susceptible to speaking words that are hurtful, deceitful, or dishonoring.

In Psalm 17:3, we gain insight into the steadfast resolve of King David regarding the use of his words. David, known for his deep spiritual insights and intimate relationship with God, expresses a profound commitment within his heart concerning the integrity of his speech.

> *Psalms 17:3 (ESV) You have tried my heart, you have visited me by night, you have tested me, and you will find nothing; I have purposed that my mouth will not transgress.*

David's declaration in Psalm 17:3 reflects a deliberate decision to guard his mouth against sinning—not only against God but also against others and himself. This intentional commitment underscores David's recognition of the weightiness of speech and its potential to either honor God or cause harm to others and oneself.

David's purposeful resolve signifies his awareness of the profound impact of words on relationships, both with God and with fellow human beings. He understands that speech has the power to build up or tear down, to encourage or discourage, to convey truth or falsehood.

In essence, David's declaration in Psalm 17:3 serves as a timeless reminder of the importance of exercising wisdom, discernment, and self-control in the use of our words. It challenges us to consider the impact of our speech on others and to purposefully align our words with the values and principles of God's Word and character.

In James 1:26, we encounter a profound admonition regarding the significance of our speech. The verse underscores the gravity of the words that flow from our lips and urges us to recognize their weightiness in shaping our character and relationships.

BE HEALED

> *James 1:26 (ESV) If anyone thinks he is religious and does not bridle his tongue but deceives his heart, this person's religion is worthless.*

James highlights the inherent connection between the heart and the mouth, emphasizing that what we speak reflects what resides within us. Our words serve as a window into the depths of our souls, revealing our thoughts, beliefs, and attitudes. They are not merely superficial expressions but rather profound reflections of our innermost being.

By emphasizing the connection between the heart and the mouth, James underscores the intimate relationship between our internal disposition and external expression. He highlights the inseparable link emphasizing that the condition of our hearts inevitably manifests through our speech.

James' exhortation serves as a sobering reminder of the responsibility we bear for the words we utter. It challenges us to examine the motives behind our speech and to consider the impact of our words on others. Why do we say what we say? James encourages us to cultivate a heart that is aligned with God's truth, love, and righteousness, so that our speech may reflect His character.

In Ephesians 4:29, the Apostle Paul imparts a profound directive regarding the significance of our speech. He presents a transformative perspective on the power of words, urging believers to wield their speech as a force for building up rather than tearing down.

> *Ephesians 4:29 (ESV) Let no corrupting talk come out of your mouths, but only such as is good for building up, as fits the occasion, that it may give grace to those who hear.*

Paul's exhortation emphasizes a shift in perspective from allowing our words to be tools of destruction, manipulated by the enemy to undermine God's authority and influence. The apostle Paul tells us to intentionally use our words to edify and strengthen the body of Christ. He underscores the responsibility entrusted to believers in shaping the Christian community through the constructive power of Godly speech.

Central to Paul's instruction is the recognition that the words we speak are a direct reflection of the condition of our hearts. He emphasizes that our speech serves as a mirror reflecting the inner landscape of our souls. Therefore, the quality and character of our words are intimately linked to the state of our hearts.

Paul underscores the principle that we can only impart to others what we possess within ourselves. In other words, the content of our speech is a direct outflow of the beliefs, values, and attitudes that permeate our hearts. Consequently, if we desire to speak words of life, encouragement, and grace, we must first cultivate a reservoir of these virtues within our own hearts. Paul's admonition in Ephesians 4:29 challenges believers to approach speech with intentionality and mindfulness. In essence, this verse serves us as a rallying cry to steward our speech wisely.

In 1 Peter 3:10, we find a promise that resonates with profound implications for our lives: the assurance of good days when we diligently guard our words and confessions. This verse explains a timeless truth that transcends circumstances and speaks to the transformative power and authority of our speech.

BE HEALED

1 Peter 3:10 (ESV) For "Whoever desires to love life and see good days, let him keep his tongue from evil and his lips from speaking deceit;

Peter's exhortation underscores the intimate connection between the quality of our days and the content of our confessions. He invites believers to recognize the profound influence of their words in shaping the future of their lives. By urging vigilance over our confessions, Peter emphasizes the importance of aligning our speech with the principles of God's truth, love, and righteousness.

The promise of good days articulated in 1 Peter 3:10 is not merely a passive assurance but a call to intentional stewardship of our speech. It beckons believers to cultivate a culture of faith and thanksgiving in their verbal expressions. By choosing to speak life, hope, and encouragement, believers invite the manifestation of God's blessings and favor into their lives.

Central to Peter's instruction is the recognition that our confessions reflect our faith and trust in God's promises. The words we speak serve as a declaration of our beliefs, values, and convictions. Therefore, by guarding our confessions and aligning them with the truth of God's Word, we actively participate with the Father in creating a reality that reflects His goodness and faithfulness.

Peter's admonition challenges believers to exercise discernment and mindfulness in their speech. It prompts us to consider the impact of our words on our own well-being, as well as on the lives of those around us. By cultivating a habit of speaking life and blessing, believers not only experience the fulfillment of God's promise of good days but also become agents of His love, mercy, and grace in the world.

In every circumstance, there exists the potential for wrong confession to take root causing despair and death to flow from our lips. However, we possess the power to choose a different path—to intentionally speak life over our situations and the circumstances around us. The act of speaking life is a conscious decision to infuse our words with hope, encouragement, and positivity, even in the face of adversity. Our words become a beacon of light in the midst of darkness, offering comfort, strength, and inspiration to those who are struggling.

Speaking life from God's Word is an expression of our identity as bearers of God's image and agents of His grace in the world. It reflects our commitment to aligning our words with His truth and His purposes, and it serves as a tangible demonstration of His love and compassion to those around us.

The choice to speak life is a lifestyle practice that has the potential to shift atmospheres, change perspectives, and bring about lasting Christlikeness in our lives and the lives of others. It is a reminder of the inherent power of our words and the profound impact they can have on the world around us. As we embrace this practice, may we be conduits of hope, healing, and restoration, speaking life into every situation we encounter in the name of our Lord Jesus Christ.

Chapter 6
UNGODLY SOUL TIES CAN CAUSE SICKNESS, ILLNESS, DISEASE, AND DEATH

Soul ties, also referred to as emotional or mental strongholds, or described as having "familiar spirits," represent a deeply entrenched issue, particularly evident among Vietnam Veterans. The experiences endured during their time in Vietnam often resulted in the development of profound emotional, mental, and physical connections known as soul ties. Unfortunately, contemporary medical approaches primarily focus on medicating symptoms rather than addressing the root cause of these soul ties.

For many Vietnam Veterans, the soul ties forged in the war have left damaging imprints on their soulish man. These ties are often accompanied by "triggers"—sights, smells, or sounds—that serve as potent flash, transporting them mentally and emotionally back to the harrowing realities of battle and the painful memories of losing comrades on the battlefield.

These triggers, often unexpected and uncontrollable, have the power to spark intense emotional and psychological responses, plunging veterans into states of distress and turmoil reminiscent of their wartime experiences. Despite the passage of time and the distance from the battlefield, the grip of these soul ties remains formidable, exerting a profound influence over the lives and well-being of those affected.

The concept of soul ties extends beyond individual experiences and can manifest in close relationships, where individuals share deep emotional connections that transcend mere physical proximity. These ties, rooted in the realm of thoughts and emotions, can give rise to a multitude of diseases and afflictions that affect not only one individual but also those closely connected to them.

Consider the case of a Christian man whose struggles with loving his wife reveal emotional and mental ties from of a past relationship. Despite being married for eight years, he found himself unable to fully embrace his wife emotionally and mentally. This difficulty stemmed from unresolved feelings and thoughts tied to his high school sweetheart, who had broken his heart years before he met his current spouse.

The pain of rejection and heartbreak inflicted by his high school sweetheart left an unmovable stronghold on his soulish man, creating soul ties that continued to influence his present relationships. Though he attempted to move forward with his life, the wounds from his past remained unhealed, shaping his perceptions and interactions with his wife.

The presence of these soul ties complicated the dynamics of his marriage and hindered the depth of intimacy and connection that should naturally flourish between spouses. His inability to fully engage with his wife emotionally stemmed from the unresolved emotions and attachments that remain tethered to his past relationship.

In his attempts to confront the issue of this soul tie, it became apparent that mere determination and willpower was insufficient to break free from its hold. Healing and restoration require a deliberate and intentional process of addressing the underlying emotional wounds and traumas that fuel these ties.

BE HEALED

Through counseling, prayer of deliverance, and spiritual guidance, individuals can break these strongholds and begin to untangle the knots of past hurts and resentments, allowing for the emergence of healthier patterns of relating and connecting with others. By acknowledging the reality of soul ties and their impact on our lives, individuals can take spiritual steps toward healing and wholeness, and reclaiming authority over their emotional and relational well-being.

The story of this man serves as a sober reminder of the profound influence of soul ties on our relationships and well-being. It underscores the importance of confronting past hurts and traumas with courage and vulnerability overcoming by the blood of the Lamb, the power of the Holy Spirit and the Word of God.

The traumatic event this man experienced not only left an imprint on his thoughts and emotions but also manifested physically in the form of ulcers and high blood pressure. The constant mental fixation on his past relationship with another woman, who had rejected him, created a barrier to him loving his wife correctly and in alignment with Biblical principles. The weight of guilt stemming from his lingering thoughts and emotions tore him apart, complicating his attempts to maintain a healthy and fulfilling marriage.

Seeking resolution and healing, he reached out for support, embarking on a journey of prayer and ministry. During a dedicated session, he confronted the soul tie that bound him to his high school sweetheart, recognizing its detrimental impact on his marriage, well-being, and his Christian testimony. Through prayer and spiritual intervention, the soul tie was severed, releasing him from its grip and ushering in a profound transformation.

The effects of this spiritual breakthrough were not confined to his emotional and relational realms but extended to his physical health as well. As the soul tie was broken, he experienced a remarkable restoration of his physical health, evidenced by the alleviation of his ulcers and high blood pressure.

The healing experienced by this man and his wife serves as a powerful testament to the redemptive power of spiritual intervention and the importance of addressing soul ties in the context of relationships. Through the dissolution of the soul tie, barriers to intimacy and connection within the marriage were dismantled, paving the way for a renewed sense of love, understanding, and partnership between husband and wife.

The wife's testimony of feeling profoundly loved for the first time in their marriage strengthens the necessity of addressing underlying spiritual and emotional wounds. It speaks to the potential for healing and restoration when individuals confront the root causes of relational strife and seek God's intervention in their lives.

This real-life example exemplifies the relevance and significance of passages of Scripture that address the complexities of human relationships and the spiritual dynamics at play. It highlights the importance of seeking wisdom, guidance, and support in navigating the complexities of marriage and interpersonal connections, recognizing that true healing often requires a spiritual approach that encompasses the spiritual, emotional, mental, and physical dimensions of human experience.

> *Psalms 1:1-3 (ESV) Blessed is the man who walks not in the counsel of the wicked, nor stands in the way of sinners, nor sits in the seat of scoffers; 2 but his delight is in the law of the LORD, and on his law he*

meditates day and night. 3 He is like a tree planted by streams of water that yields its fruit in its season, and its leaf does not wither. In all that he does, he prospers.

The word blessed in Psalms 1 means inner happiness and under the favor of God. The three things we are not to do or have, according to Psalms 1, include.

- *UNGODLY ADVICE*
- *UNGODLY ASSOCIATES*
- *UNGODLY ATTACKERS*

What Can We Do?

In Psalms 1, we encounter profound wisdom concerning the principles of relationships and associations that shape our lives. Adherence to these principles unlocks God's favor, leading to the manifestation of the fruit of happiness and fulfillment. However, disobedience to these principles invites God's displeasure and establishes soul ties with the wicked or ungodly, setting the stage for the unfolding of the consequences outlined in the rest of Psalms 1.

The psalmist presents a contrast between the righteous and the wicked, highlighting the distinct paths they choose to follow. Those who delight in God's law and meditate on it day and night are likened to flourishing trees planted by streams of water, yielding fruit in season, and prospering in all they do. Their lives are characterized by stability, productivity, and inner peace, reflecting the redemptive power of aligning oneself with God's truth and wisdom.

However, those who reject God's law and embrace ungodly counsel are depicted as chaff blown away by the wind, devoid of substance and purpose. Their lives are marked by instability, emptiness, and ultimate destruction, as they forsake the path of righteousness in pursuit of fleeting pleasures and worldly pursuits.

The principles outlined in Psalms 1 underscore the profound impact of our choices and associations on our spiritual well-being and ultimate destiny. By cultivating a heart that delights in God's truth and wisdom, we position ourselves to receive His favor and blessings.

On the contrary, to disregard God's law and align oneself with the ways of the wicked is to invite spiritual impoverishment and separation from God's presence. The establishment of soul ties with the ungodly compromises our spiritual integrity and hinders our ability to experience the fullness of God's purpose and provision in our lives.

In essence, Psalms 1 serves as a timeless reminder of the importance of intentional and discerning living, rooted in Jesus Christ, having a deep reverence for God's Word, and a commitment to walk in in the power of the Holy Spirit. It beckons us to consider the implications of our choices and associations, recognizing that our relationships shape our character and influence our spiritual journey. Remember, bad company ruins good morals. As we embrace the principles of righteousness outlined in Psalms 1, may we experience the richness of God's favor and the abundance of His blessings in every area of our lives.

> *Psalms 1:4-6 (ESV) The wicked are not so, but are like chaff that the wind drives away. 5 Therefore the wicked will not stand in the judgment, nor sinners in the congregation of the righteous; 6 for the LORD*

knows the way of the righteous, but the way of the wicked will perish.

As we engage with the Scriptures, it is essential to be attentive to the presence of soul ties—those connections or associations that bind individuals to influences contrary to God's will. These soul ties often lead people to become entangled with the "wrong crowd," resulting in profound changes in their soul, physical health, and spiritual well-being. Recognizing and acknowledging these soul ties is a critical step toward experiencing healing and restoration.

Throughout the Scriptures, we encounter numerous instances where individuals formed connections that had a significant impact on their lives. In many cases, these connections lead them astray from God's purposes, causing them to compromise their values and beliefs. Whether through unhealthy relationships, ungodly influences, or sinful patterns of behavior, soul ties can exert a powerful hold on individuals, shaping their thoughts, emotions, and actions in ways that are contrary to God's truth and leaving a proper testimony of Christ living in us.

The process of confessing and renouncing these soul ties is a vital component of the healing journey. It involves acknowledging the presence of these ties and their detrimental effects on one's life, as well as seeking God's forgiveness and cleansing. Confession opens the door to restoration, allowing individuals to break free from the grip of unhealthy relationships and negative influences and to experience the fullness of God's grace and healing.

Healing from soul ties encompasses not only the spiritual realm but also the soul and physical body. It involves addressing the wounds and scars left behind by past connections, allowing God's power to bring healing and wholeness to every aspect of one's being in Jesus' name. Through prayer, repentance, and intentionality to align oneself with God's will and Word, individuals can experience profound healing and restoration from the damaging effects of soul ties.

> *James 5:16 (ESV) Therefore, confess your sins to one another and pray for one another, that you may be healed. The prayer of a righteous person has great power as it is working.*

James 5:16 offers profound insights into the healing power of confession and prayer within the body of Christ. While we understand that confession of our sins before the Lord leads to forgiveness, James emphasizes an additional dimension: the healing that comes from confessing our faults to one another.

In acknowledging our sins before God, we experience the assurance of His forgiveness and restoration. However, the act of confessing our sins to fellow believers carries with it a unique dynamic—one that fosters healing and wholeness in multiple dimensions: emotional, mental, and physical.

The process of confessing our faults to others creates a space of humility, vulnerability, and accountability within the fellowship of believers. It requires brokenness, humility, and transparency as we lay bare our struggles and shortcomings before trusted brothers and sisters in Christ. In this environment of trust and support, the weight of guilt and shame is lifted, and the healing balm of grace is applied to wounded hearts and minds.

The act of confession before others serves as a means for emotional healing, providing an outlet for pent-up emotions and anxieties. By verbalizing our struggles and burdens, we release the internalized tension and find solace in the empathy and understanding of our fellow believers. We move from having peace with our Lord Jesus Christ to a deep sense of peace and fellowship with our Christian brothers and sisters in the Lord.

Moreover, the mental healing that accompanies confession stems from the reassurance of God's unconditional love and acceptance, forgiveness that is found in our Lord Jesus, and the Biblical compassion of our Christian family, In this context of grace and forgiveness, individuals experience a renewed sense of peace and clarity of mind, liberated from the grip of guilt and self-condemnation.

In essence, James 5:16 invites believers into a sacred practice of confession and mutual support, fostering a safe environment of grace, healing, and restoration within the Church family.

In my extensive ministry spanning over 47 years, I've witnessed numerous instances where disagreements over doctrine or church governance led people to leave our church community. I can empathize with this phenomenon because I, too, have departed from churches due to doctrinal or governance differences. However, one aspect that continues to puzzle me is the phenomenon of soul ties.

Here it is. When an individual disagrees with me on matters of doctrine or governance and decides to leave the church, it often triggers a ripple effect. Not only does that person depart, but also those who are connected to them in any way—whether family members or friends—tend to follow suit. It's as if there's a spiritual bond that extends beyond mere agreement on matters of faith or church practices.

What baffles me is that the decision to leave seems to extend past individual convictions or assessments of the Word of God and church administration. It appears that there's a soul tie binding together a group of individuals, based on family or social connections, that supersedes their consideration for Biblical truth. Despite past differing opinions or hostilities within the group, the influence of this soul tie remains strong, leading them to depart collectively. The group is bond together because they have a common enemy, the pastor.

The Lord's warning about this phenomenon being significant in the end times resonates deeply with me. It's a sobering reminder that as we prioritize the truth of God's Word and uphold sound doctrine, we may encounter resistance even from within our own households. Breaking the grip of family soul ties and placing the Word of truth above all else can be a challenging and painful process, often leading to conflict and division among loved ones.

As we continue to journey through these end times, let us remain vigilant and prayerful, seeking wisdom and discernment as we navigate the intricate dynamics of relationships and spiritual warfare. May our unwavering devotion to God's truth serve as a beacon of light amidst the darkness, illuminating the path of righteousness for ourselves and those around us.

> *Matthew 10:34-39 (ESV) "Do not think that I have come to bring peace to the earth. I have not come to bring peace, but a sword. 35 For I have come to set a man against his father, and a daughter against her mother, and a daughter-in-law against her mother-in-law. 36 And a person's enemies will be those of his own household. 37 Whoever loves father or mother more than me is not worthy of me, and whoever loves*

son or daughter more than me is not worthy of me. 38 And whoever does not take his cross and follow me is not worthy of me. 39 Whoever finds his life will lose it, and whoever loses his life for my sake will find it.

Soul ties have the insidious power to keep us trapped in defeat and frustration, leading to ungodly patterns of thought and behavior. They can ensnare us in fantasies, daydreams, and desires for relationships outside of our mate and our Lord Jesus Christ. These ties are not limited to individuals but can extend to religious items such as denominations or physical structures like church buildings.

I've encountered individuals who cling so tightly to their denomination or church building that they prioritize it above their spiritual well-being. Some have expressed a willingness to sacrifice their spiritual growth rather than part with the manmade teachings their religious affiliation. This level of attachment can foster idolatry, witchcraft, and religious spirits, blinding individuals to the true essence of their faith.

As a pastor, I've witnessed firsthand the detrimental effects of soul ties to church buildings. Some individuals become so enamored with the physical structure that they prioritize it over genuine relationships and spiritual growth. They build an idol by exalting the edifice above their worship of the Father, Son, or Holy Spirit. Their attachment to the building eclipses their love for the Lord, leading to a trail of broken relationships and hurt individuals in their wake.

In essence, soul ties can distort our priorities and lead us astray from the true essence of faith. They can foster unhealthy attachments and behaviors that hinder our spiritual growth and alienate us from authentic Christian community and fellowship. Recognizing and breaking free from these ties is essential for experiencing true freedom and fulfillment in our relationship with God and others.

If you believe you're entangled in an unhealthy soul tie that disrupts your thoughts and feelings, seek guidance from a Christian spiritual leader who comprehends such matters and engage in prayer ministry. There ought to be a discernible separation, both natural and supernatural, between what is pure and what is corrupted, between the wheat and the tares. Like trees firmly rooted by flowing streams, we should avoid forming soul ties with those who embody wickedness.

I cherished and respected my father, who has transitioned into eternity. I find solace in the fact that he professed faith in our Lord Jesus Christ two years before his passing. Despite my deep love and respect for him as my father, prior to his salvation, I couldn't fellowship with him so as not to establish an unhealthy soul tie. His actions didn't align with God's ways, and his beliefs and declarations differed from those of my heavenly Father. Consequently, we remained distant in the spiritual and soulish realm for the majority of my Christian journey.

Choosing to prioritize truth and my relationship with my heavenly Father over seeking peace with my dad was not an easy decision. Was it straightforward? Certainly not!

Similar situations arose in the past with certain church members who invited me to one of their grip sessions. They urged me to refrain from raising my hands, applauding before the Lord, and standing during the music during the church services. Additionally, I was advised to reduce my preaching about the ways and actions of the ministry of the Person of the Holy Spirit.

They warned that if I persisted, they would sever fellowship and leave the church. It hasn't been a smooth journey, but I opt to align myself with God rather than with man. This decision has resulted in breaking fellowship with individuals who departed from our church services. However, in preventing the formation of soul ties, we must determine whom we aim to please. Will we dedicate our time and efforts to pleasing people or pleasing God?

Perhaps the most notable and powerful soul tie I've observed occurs between a parent and their son or daughter after marriage. The Bible instructs us to "leave and cleave," yet repeatedly, I witness unhealthy dynamics between the spouse and one or both of their parents. The most prevalent scenario I encounter involves the new wife and her mother or the new husband and his mother.

> *Matthew 10:21 (ESV) Brother will deliver brother over to death, and the father his child, and children will rise against parents and have them put to death,*
>
> *Matthew 12:46-50 (ESV) While he was still speaking to the people, behold, his mother and his brothers stood outside, asking to speak to him. 48 But he replied to the man who told him, "Who is my mother, and who are my brothers?" 49 And stretching out his hand toward his disciples, he said, "Here are my mother and my brothers! 50 For whoever does the will of my Father in heaven is my brother and sister and mother."*

What Can I Do To Cancel And Break Soul Ties?

To cancel and break soul ties, I must embark on a journey of redefining my concept of family. This task represents one of the most intricate decisions and challenging positions to uphold. I find myself most closely connected with individuals who are committed to fulfilling the will of my heavenly Father. It's been a recurring experience where family members, whether from my side or my wife's, have felt like mere acquaintances, sensing a disconnection from me due to my adherence to the Word of God.

> *2 Corinthians 6:14-17 (ESV) Do not be unequally yoked with unbelievers. For what partnership has righteousness with lawlessness? Or what fellowship has light with darkness? 15 What accord has Christ with Belial? Or what portion does a believer share with an unbeliever? 16 What agreement has the temple of God with idols? For we are the temple of the living God; as God said, "I will make my dwelling among them and walk among them, and I will be their God, and they shall be my people. 17 Therefore go out from their midst, and be separate from them, says the Lord, and touch no unclean thing; then I will welcome you,*

In 1 Corinthians 6:14-17, our Lord's message is crystal clear: there's an inherent issue with mixing incompatible elements, much like attempting to blend water with gasoline or oil with water. The stark contrast between darkness and light underscores the impossibility of coexistence in the same space; one must inevitably yield to the other. Thus, what sort of fellowship, or soul tie, can a believer truly share with a nonbeliever? How can righteousness and unrighteousness peacefully cohabit? The answer lies in taking decisive action to prevent the establishment of such soul ties: ***"Come out from among them!"*** This biblical injunction urges believers to separate themselves from environments and relationships that compromise their faith.

BE HEALED

By delving into Scripture, one can discern instances of soul ties, moments where individuals became entangled with the wrong crowd, leading to detrimental changes in their emotional, physical, and spiritual well-being. A perfect example is found in the story of Joshua's unwitting alliance with the Gibeonites (See Joshua 9), illustrating the consequences of forming alliances without discernment and wisdom.

Canceling And Breaking Soul Ties

- *The best way is not to enter into an agreement or covenant with someone spiritually lost or a believer not walking with the Lord.*
- *Confess any ungodly or unhealthy soul ties and get forgiveness. Commit to walk according to the Word, especially in the marriage relationship.*
- *Be warned and know the dangers of entering into friendship with the world and those of the world.*
- *Be active in taking back the ground (spiritually, emotionally, mentally, physically, or financially) given up in ignorance.*
- *Learn to possess your body and soul as vessels of honor.*

   3 John 1:2 (ESV) Beloved, I pray that all may go well with you and that you may be in good health, as it goes well with your soul.

Chapter 7
DEMONIC PRESENCE IN THE WAY OF OPPRESSION OR POSSESSION CAN CAUSE SICKNESS, ILLNESS, DISEASE, AND DEATH

A demonic presence, often referred to as "demon possession" or "demon oppression," denotes a condition where individuals are subject to the influence or intrusion of demonic spiritual forces. It's important to clarify that when we use the term "possession," we don't imply ownership as commonly understood today. Rather, it signifies a state where demonic activity encroaches upon an individual's rights and autonomy, akin to trespassing on their spiritual and emotional boundaries.

In the realm of deliverance ministry, a significant observation emerged: more than fifty percent of Multiple Sclerosis (MS) patients experienced healing from their condition following the expulsion of demonic entities. This underscores the profound impact that spiritual intervention can have on physical ailments, revealing the intricate interplay between spiritual and bodily well-being.

It's crucial to understand that if you, a family member, or a friend are grappling with Multiple Sclerosis (MS), the observation I've made over the years doesn't imply that your condition is necessarily influenced by demonic presence. What I'm highlighting is that in more than fifty percent of the cases where individuals sought prayer and deliverance from me, there was a correlation between their struggles with MS and the presence of demonic entities.

BE HEALED

Job: The Righteous Man And Godly Father

When delving into the relationship between demonic influence and various aspects of suffering such as sickness, illness, disease, afflictions, and even death, it's imperative to revisit the narrative of our friend Job from the Scriptures.

> *Job 1:1 (ESV) There was a man in the land of Uz whose name was Job, and that man was blameless and upright, one who feared God and turned away from evil.*

Job's story serves as a profound illustration of the complexities surrounding human suffering and the interplay between spiritual and physical realms. Despite his righteousness and devotion to God, Job endured immense trials, including the loss of his wealth, health, and even the lives of his loved ones. His afflictions encompassed physical ailments, emotional distress, and spiritual anguish. All of this was the work of the demonic.

In Job 1:1, we encounter a profound description of Job's character encased in the words, "that man was blameless and upright, one who feared God and turned away from evil." This single sentence weaves together four powerful expressions that paint a vivid picture of Job's integrity and devotion to God.

- *Job was blameless*
- *Job was upright*
- *Job feared God*
- *Job turned away from evil*

Throughout the narrative, we witness the dialogue between Job and his friends as they grapple with the theological implications of his suffering. Job's friends initially attributed his misfortunes to divine punishment for undisclosed sins.

The language employed in Job 1:1 offers a profound insight into Job's character, portraying him as complete, mature, and fully developed in every aspect, leaving no room for gaps or flaws. This description underscores Job's impeccable integrity and moral uprightness, suggesting that he was above reproach in his conduct and demeanor.

It's crucial to note, however, that Job's righteousness and goodness do not imply an absence of sin. Rather, they signify his deep reverence, obedience, and gratitude toward God. Job's piety was evident in his unwavering commitment to living a life aligned with divine principles, even amidst the temptations and trials of the world.

Job's religious devotion was akin to wearing a white garment untainted by the pleasures and corruptions of the world. His faith was not merely a superficial adornment but a deeply ingrained aspect of his identity, manifesting in his words, actions, and interactions with others. Through his steadfast adherence to God's commandments and his unwavering trust in divine providence, Job exemplified the essence of true faith and righteousness.

> *Job 1:2 (ESV) There were born to him seven sons and three daughters.*
>
> *Job 1:3 (ESV) He possessed 7,000 sheep, 3,000 camels, 500 yoke of oxen, and 500 female donkeys, and very many servants, so that this man was the greatest of all the people of the east.*

It appears that Job experienced a period of uninterrupted prosperity throughout his adult years. His children had reached maturity, and there is no indication that he ever faced financial hardship. Despite his abundant wealth, Job did not flaunt his riches over others; instead, he humbly embraced the blessings of financial abundance. Additionally, Job enjoyed the richness of relational blessings, with his grown children continuing to surround him, fostering a close-knit family atmosphere.

Job found great satisfaction in the continual growth of his flocks, including sheep, camels, oxen, and donkeys, which grazed in lush pastures. Beyond his thriving livestock, Job possessed extensive land, a sizable family, numerous servants, and the financial resources to maintain a comfortable lifestyle. Moreover, both Job and his family experienced robust health, adding to their overall well-being.

To observers, it might seem as though Job lived a life of unparalleled abundance, with all the trappings of wealth and prosperity. From the outside looking in, some might even view Job as having been born with a proverbial silver spoon in his mouth, possessing everything that many could only dream of or aspire to attain.

In the narrative of Job, one notable absence from his life was the experience of trials, tribulations, sickness, afflictions, and death. Remarkably, there is no recorded instance of mourning in Job's life, even after the passing of his father and mother, who died of old age. Throughout his life, Job seemed to have been shielded from the various forms of suffering that often afflict humanity, including physical ailments and the loss of loved ones. This absence of adversity underscores the seemingly perfect nature of Job's existence prior to the onset of his profound trials.

Within the story, there are no documented instances of drought affecting his crops, diseases plaguing his livestock, or theft targeting his possessions. It appears that Job maintained a constant awareness of the divine providence that showered blessings upon him. His friends and acquaintances held him in high esteem, regarding him as a person of integrity and reverence, a faithful servant of the Most High God. Job's life seemed to unfold within a sphere of divine favor and protection, shielded from many of the adversities that commonly befall individuals. This recognition of Job's unshakable faith and moral character underscores the depth of his relationship with the Divine and the esteem in which he was held by those around him.

> *Job 1:4-5 (ESV) His sons used to go and hold a feast in the house of each one on his day, and they would send and invite their three sisters to eat and drink with them. 5 And when the days of the feast had run their course, Job would send and consecrate them, and he would rise early in the morning and offer burnt offerings according to the number of them all. For Job said, "It may be that my children have sinned, and cursed God in their hearts." Thus Job did continually.*

In the story of Job, we learn that each of his seven sons took turns hosting gatherings where they entertained one another. While it's plausible that these events were birthday celebrations, the Bible doesn't explicitly state their purpose, leaving room for speculation. Nevertheless, at the conclusion of these gatherings, Job made a habit of offering sacrifices on behalf of his family, perhaps as a precautionary measure in case any of his sons inadvertently sinned during the festivities.

This scene paints a beautiful picture of what appears to be a harmonious and joyous family life within the household of Job. Despite the absence of any indication that

Job's sons were engaged in ungodly activities during these gatherings, Job's commitment to offering sacrifices reflects his thoughtful and conscientious approach to ensuring the spiritual well-being of his family. Rather than responding to specific wrongdoing, Job's actions exemplify a mindset of erring on the side of caution, demonstrating his deep concern for the spiritual integrity of his loved ones.

As we immerse ourselves in the book of Job, we discern that Job's speeches frequently reflect his unwavering commitment to the Most High God. It becomes evident that his righteous conduct towards his fellow men was deeply rooted in his profound belief in a just and generous Creator. Despite residing in a community where worship of the sun and moon prevailed, Job steadfastly abstained from participating in such practices, remaining resolute in his devotion to the One True God.

Job's commitment to his faith amidst cultural pressures and societal norms highlights the strength of his convictions and the depth of his spiritual integrity. His steadfast refusal to compromise his beliefs serves as a witness to his unwavering commitment to serving and honoring God, even in the face of adversity and opposition. Through Job's example, we glean invaluable insights into the importance of standing firm in our convictions and remaining faithful to our beliefs, regardless of the prevailing cultural currents, social moral collapses or evil influences.

The narrative of Job commences with an introduction to his family, comprising his wife, seven sons, and three daughters. Together, they reside in a state of abundance and prosperity, enjoying the blessings of their collective fortunes. Job's household stands as a testament to his success and stature within his community, symbolizing not only material wealth but also harmony and unity within the family structure. Within the context of their family dynamics, Job's wife and children play integral roles in the unfolding narrative.

> *Job 1:6-8 (ESV) Now there was a day when the sons of God came to present themselves before the LORD, and Satan also came among them. 7 The LORD said to Satan, "From where have you come?" Satan answered the LORD and said, "From going to and fro on the earth, and from walking up and down on it." 8 And the LORD said to Satan, "Have you considered my servant Job, that there is none like him on the earth, a blameless and upright man, who fears God and turns away from evil?"*

In Job 1:6-8, we are granted a glimpse into the heavenly realm, where a profound dialogue unfolds between God and Satan. The imagery presented paints a vivid picture of Satan's restless demeanor, as he describes himself as "going to and fro in the earth, and pacing up and down in it." This portrayal suggests that Satan has taken upon himself a task akin to observing humanity, perhaps vigilant for their misdeeds or vulnerabilities.

Satan emerges as a figure characterized by relentless curiosity and acute scrutiny of human lives and motives. His restless spirit and keen eye for weaknesses reflect a relentless quest to exploit human frailties and vulnerabilities. Moreover, Satan's propensity to quickly imagine evil underscores the depth of his wicked nature and his relentless pursuit of discord and destruction.

The scene in heaven serves as a compelling backdrop for the unfolding drama of Job's trials and tribulations, illustrating the cosmic dimensions of the spiritual conflict between good and evil. Through this dialogue, we gain insight into the battle between God's divine sovereignty and the forces of darkness, setting the stage for the profound themes of suffering, faith, and redemption that characterize the narrative of Job.

> *Job 1:9-11 (ESV) Then Satan answered the LORD and said, "Does Job fear God for no reason? 10 Have you not put a hedge around him and his house and all that he has, on every side? You have blessed the work of his hands, and his possessions have increased in the land. 11 But stretch out your hand and touch all that he has, and he will curse you to your face."*

We should notice in Job 1:9-11 that Satan was unable to inflict harm on Job or his family without God's permission.

> *Job 1:12 (ESV) And the LORD said to Satan, "Behold, all that he has is in your hand. Only against him do not stretch out your hand." So Satan went out from the presence of the LORD.*

In Job 1:12, we encounter a pivotal moment where God sets boundaries on the extent to which trials, tribulations, and afflictions inflicted by the demonic forces can impact Job's life. Despite granting Satan permission to afflict Job's servants and family members, God imposes a crucial limitation: Satan is prohibited from taking Job's life.

This divine intervention highlights the intricate balance between God's divine sovereignty and human suffering. While Job is subjected to immense trials and losses, including the devastating loss of his loved ones and servants, God's protective hand prevents the ultimate tragedy of Job's own demise.

God oversees the lives of His faithful servants. Even amidst the most harrowing of circumstances, God's sovereignty remains unshaken, offering hope and assurance amid the storms of life.

The Thief Of Livestock And Death Of Job's Servants

> *Job 1:13-15 (ESV) Now there was a day when his sons and daughters were eating and drinking wine in their oldest brother's house, 14 and there came a messenger to Job and said, "The oxen were plowing and the donkeys feeding beside them, 15 and the Sabeans fell upon them and took them and struck down the servants with the edge of the sword, and I alone have escaped to tell you."*

Satan And Sickness

Satan operates within strict confines determined by the Almighty, rendering him subject to divine governance. His ability to inflict harm is contingent upon obtaining permission, highlighting the overseeing control of God's wisdom and goodness over evil itself.

Granted permission to deceive and tempt, Satan crafts circumstances designed to undermine Job in every way and to test his faith in God. The strategies of the enemy extended beyond mere external events. Satan employed persuasive arguments from Job's friends aimed at distorting his moral truths, seeking to portray evil as good and good as evil. Despite his wicked intentions, Satan's actions serve a greater purpose. He orchestrated trials against Job's faith and steadfastness.

Job 2:6-7 (ESV) And the LORD said to Satan, "Behold, he is in your hand; only spare his life." 7 So Satan went out from the presence of the LORD and struck Job with loathsome sores from the sole of his foot to the crown of his head.

In Job 2:6-7, we witness the distressing manifestation of Satan's wicked influence on Job's physical well-being. Satan, given permission by God to afflict Job, inflicts upon him severe and excruciating skin boils that cover his body from head to toe.

These boils represent not only physical suffering but also symbolize the depth of Job's anguish and despair. The affliction is comprehensive, leaving no part of Job's body untouched by pain and discomfort. It is a constant reminder of the profound depths of suffering that humanity can endure, particularly when subjected to the relentless onslaught of evil forces.

The image of Job covered in boils serves as a sober reminder of the reality of suffering in the world. This should prompt us to confront the questions of human suffering and divine providence that lie at the heart of the Book of Job.

It is imperative to acknowledge again that Satan, despite his wicked and evil intentions, was unable to inflict harm upon Job or his family without explicit permission from God. This crucial dynamic is clearly depicted in Job 1:7-12 and Job 2:2-6, where Satan's actions are governed by God's divine authority. Moreover, it's noteworthy that Satan was expressly prohibited from taking Job's life, underscoring the ultimate sovereignty of God over the forces of darkness.

New Testament Examples Of Sickness Caused By The Demonic

Further insights into Satan's role in sickness and affliction are provided in Acts 10:38 and various passages throughout the New Testament. Here, we witness Jesus and the apostles engaging in acts of healing and restoration, directly opposing the destructive influence of Satan.

> *Acts 10:38 (ESV) how God anointed Jesus of Nazareth with the Holy Spirit and with power. He went about doing good and healing all who were oppressed by the devil, for God was with him.*

In Luke 13:11-13, Jesus performs a miraculous healing, liberating a woman who had been crippled for eighteen years under the oppressive grip of a spirit associated with Satan.

> *Luke 13:10-13 (ESV) Now he was teaching in one of the synagogues on the Sabbath. 11 And behold, there was a woman who had had a disabling spirit for eighteen years. She was bent over and could not fully straighten herself. 12 When Jesus saw her, he called her over and said to her, "Woman, you are freed from your disability." 13 And he laid his hands on her, and immediately she was made straight, and she glorified God.*

> *Luke 13:15-16 (ESV) Then the Lord answered him, "You hypocrites! Does not each of you on the Sabbath untie his ox or his donkey from the manger and lead it away to water it? 16 And ought not this woman, a daughter of Abraham whom Satan bound*

for eighteen years, be loosed from this bond on the Sabbath day?"

These accounts illuminate the ongoing spiritual warfare between God who would represent the force of good and the demonic, who represents the force of evil. These examples highlight for us the profound implications of divine intervention in the face of suffering and affliction. Through acts of healing and restoration, Jesus and his followers confronted the demonic oppressive forces of darkness, offering hope and redemption to those ensnared by the influence of Satan. In doing so, they reaffirm the redemptive power of faith and the enduring promise of victory of God's mercy and grace over the kingdom of darkness.

Our Lord Jesus Christ cast a blind and dumb spirit out of a boy who suffered from both conditions. He also cast a mute spirit out of a man. It's crucial to note that these incidents do not imply that every individual who experiences blindness and muteness is afflicted by demonic presence. However, in these particular cases encountered by our Lord, the afflictions were indeed attributable to demonic influences. This is why we must walk in discernment and ask the Father for His wisdom and words of knowledge.

> *Matthew 9:32-33 (ESV) As they were going away, behold, a demon-oppressed man who was mute was brought to him. 33 And when the demon had been cast out, the mute man spoke. And the crowds marveled, saying, "Never was anything like this seen in Israel."*

Matthew 12:22 (ESV) Then a demon-oppressed man who was blind and mute was brought to him, and he healed him, so that the man spoke and saw.

In Mark 5:2-13, we encounter a gripping account of a man tormented by a legion of demons, so numerous that they compelled him to harm himself and break free from chains. This man, consumed by the oppressive grip of demonic possession, endured unimaginable suffering until he encountered Jesus.

Upon encountering Jesus, the demons within the man begged to be released, and Jesus granted their request, allowing them to enter a herd of pigs nearby. The sheer magnitude of the demonic presence was staggering, estimated to be as many as six thousand or more.

The consequences of this liberation were profound. The pigs, now possessed by the expelled demons, rushed into the nearby river and drowned. This dramatic event serves as a powerful demonstration of the destructive power of evil forces and the profound impact of God's divine intervention.

Mark 5:2-13 (ESV) And when Jesus had stepped out of the boat, immediately there met him out of the tombs a man with an unclean spirit. 3 He lived among the tombs. And no one could bind him anymore, not even with a chain, 4 for he had often been bound with shackles and chains, but he wrenched the chains apart, and he broke the shackles in pieces. No one had the strength to subdue him. 5 Night and day among the tombs and on the mountains he was always crying out and cutting himself with stones. 6 And when he saw Jesus from afar, he ran and fell down before him. 7 And crying out with a loud voice,

> he said, "What have you to do with me, Jesus, Son of the Most High God? I adjure you by God, do not torment me." 8 For he was saying to him, "Come out of the man, you unclean spirit!" 9 And Jesus asked him, "What is your name?" He replied, "My name is Legion, for we are many." 10 And he begged him earnestly not to send them out of the country. 11 Now a great herd of pigs was feeding there on the hillside, 12 and they begged him, saying, "Send us to the pigs; let us enter them." 13 So he gave them permission. And the unclean spirits came out and entered the pigs; and the herd, numbering about two thousand, rushed down the steep bank into the sea and drowned in the sea.

I vividly recall a young lady in her late twenties who visited our church one day—a memory etched in my mind. Her appearance spoke volumes; she embodied the Gothic culture with white face makeup, dark eyes, black hair, and clothes adorned with Gothic piercings. Her demeanor exuded rebellion, evident from a mile away. Approaching her, I asked if she would allow me to pray with her, to which she agreed wholeheartedly. As we entered into prayer, the Lord revealed to me profound insights concerning the deep-seated issues of rebellion and rejection that plagued her spirit.

I extended an invitation for her to join us at our home the following day for a time of ministry with me and my wife, to which she eagerly agreed. As she arrived the next day, my wife and I began praying earnestly over her, confronting the demonic presence that held her in bondage. Almost immediately, she began to manifest signs of demonic influence. Undeterred, we persevered in prayer and spiritual warfare for nearly two hours, sensing a breakthrough as we fervently prayed against the demonic strongholds. Eventually, we felt a shift, a sense that the oppressive forces had been shattered.

In that moment, the young lady made a heartfelt decision to accept the Lord Jesus as her Savior. A transformation swept over her countenance as the love of God enveloped her, illuminating her face with newfound peace and joy. It was a powerful testament to the redemptive power of prayer and the transformative grace of God.

The following week when she returned to church, she was virtually unrecognizable. Gone were the Gothic makeup, the edgy hairstyle, and the piercings. Instead, she was adorned like a radiant young lady, exuding a newfound sense of beauty and grace. Her excitement to share the good news with her husband, who was working abroad, was noticeable. Upon his return home, he was astounded by the remarkable difference in his wife's appearance and demeanor. He confessed to me that it felt as though he was married to an entirely different woman—a testament to the profound change that had taken place in her life.

Today, this couple is deeply engaged in serving the Lord, actively involved in teaching Bible classes, and nurturing their three beautiful children. What launched this transformative journey? It was Biblically standing against the insidious grip of demonic oppression—specifically, the strongholds of rebellion and rejection—that had ensnared her emotions and thoughts, dictating her mannerisms, speech, and behavior. When we broke these demonic strongholds, she experienced a profound shift in perspective. Liberated by the Lord Jesus Christ from the shackles of rebellion and rejection, she began to see herself through the lens of divine love and acceptance, no longer bound by the spirit of rebellion and rejection that once held her captive. This newfound clarity allowed her to embrace her true identity in Christ, paving the way for a life transformed by grace and redemption.

Other New Testament Examples

> *Matthew 8:16 (ESV) That evening they brought to him many who were oppressed by demons, and he cast out the spirits with a word and healed all who were sick.*
>
> *Mark 9:20-27 (ESV) And they brought the boy to him. And when the spirit saw him, immediately it convulsed the boy, and he fell on the ground and rolled about, foaming at the mouth. 21 And Jesus asked his father, "How long has this been happening to him?" And he said, "From childhood. 22 And it has often cast him into fire and into water, to destroy him. But if you can do anything, have compassion on us and help us." 23 And Jesus said to him, "'If you can'! All things are possible for one who believes." 24 Immediately the father of the child cried out and said, "I believe; help my unbelief!" 25 And when Jesus saw that a crowd came running together, he rebuked the unclean spirit, saying to it, "You mute and deaf spirit, I command you, come out of him and never enter him again." 26 And after crying out and convulsing him terribly, it came out, and the boy was like a corpse, so that most of them said, "He is dead." 27 But Jesus took him by the hand and lifted him up, and he arose.*
>
> *Luke 8:2 (ESV) and also some women who had been healed of evil spirits and infirmities: Mary, called Magdalene, from whom seven demons had gone out,*

What Can We Do?

In cases of affliction stemming from demonic activity, the crucial need for "deliverance" arises, aiming to release the afflicted individuals from the authority, stronghold, and bondage imposed by these evil forces. If prayer and fasting have been diligently pursued for physical, emotional, or mental healing without yielding results, seeking assistance from someone experienced in deliverance ministry becomes imperative.

Regrettably, many Christians harbor doubts regarding the effectiveness today of Biblical teachings, coupled with a deep-seated fear of engaging with the demonic realm. Consequently, they shy away from participating in prayers for those afflicted by demonic oppression. This reluctance unveils a pervasive stronghold of fear that must be addressed and dispelled to enable individuals to fully embrace the liberating power of faith and spiritual intervention.

The reluctance to confront the demonic and engage in deliverance ministry reflects a broader spiritual battle—a lack of faith. This issue necessitates a courageous and unwavering commitment to aligning with the truths of Scripture and actively combating fear with faith. Through fervent prayer, steadfast reliance on Biblical principles, and a willingness to confront spiritual strongholds, individuals can experience profound freedom from the bonds of fear and embrace the liberating power of the Father's divine deliverance.

There exists a group of believers who hold unwavering faith in the Word of God, fully embracing the truth that Christ within us is greater than any adversary in the world. Often referred to as the "Mark 16 believers," they embody a profound understanding of spiritual warfare and are equipped with the divine authority to combat the forces of darkness. Armed with the promises of Scripture and empowered by the indwelling presence of Christ and the Holy Spirit, these believers pose a formidable threat to the enemy's schemes and strategies.

Their unwavering faith serves as a beacon of hope and strength for those in need, offering a source of spiritual refuge and healing. In times of distress or spiritual warfare, seeking out these steadfast believers for prayer and support can be transformative. Their prayers are infused with the authority and power of the Holy Spirit, capable of breaking chains, dispelling darkness, and ushering in the light of divine grace and restoration.

Encountering a Mark 16 believer is akin to encountering a spiritual warrior—an individual whose faith is unshakeable, whose prayers are fervent, and whose commitment to advancing God's kingdom is unwavering. In their presence, the presence of God is tangible, offering solace, strength, and renewed hope to all who seek their counsel and intercession.

> *Mark 16:17-18 (ESV) And these signs will accompany those who believe: in my name they will cast out demons; they will speak in new tongues; 18 they will pick up serpents with their hands; and if they drink any deadly poison, it will not hurt them; they will lay their hands on the sick, and they will recover."*
>
> *Mark 16:20 (ESV) And they went out and preached everywhere, while the Lord worked with them and confirmed the message by accompanying signs.]]*

Our Area Of Influence

What about those who try to heal and cast out demons but do not have the right or faith to do so?

> *Acts 19:13 (ESV) Then some of the itinerant Jewish exorcists undertook to invoke the name of the Lord Jesus over those who had evil spirits, saying, "I adjure you by the Jesus whom Paul proclaims."*

> *Acts 19:14-18 (ESV) Seven sons of a Jewish high priest named Sceva were doing this. 15 But the evil spirit answered them, "Jesus I know, and Paul I recognize, but who are you?" 16 And the man in whom was the evil spirit leaped on them, mastered all of them and overpowered them, so that they fled out of that house naked and wounded. 17 And this became known to all the residents of Ephesus, both Jews and Greeks. And fear fell upon them all, and the name of the Lord Jesus was extolled. 18 Also many of those who were now believers came, confessing and divulging their practices.*

The seriousness of spiritual warfare cannot be overstated, yet it appears to have been trivialized in certain Christian circles. I've encountered instances where individuals speak of casting demons into hell or binding demonic activity across the entire earth. However, it's crucial to address our collective ignorance of Biblical truth in these matters.

First and foremost, we must recognize that we do not possess the authority to banish demons to hell. Such authority lies solely with our Lord, who will exercise judgment over all things at the culmination of time. Therefore, our attempts to sound spiritually profound by casting demons into hell are misguided and lack Biblical foundation.

Similarly, the notion of binding demonic spirits or activity over the earth is based on wishful thinking and borders on religious folly. We must acknowledge the limitations of our authority and refrain from engaging in actions that exceed our spiritual jurisdiction.

Instead of relying on sensationalized practices, we ought to seek a deeper understanding of Biblical principles regarding spiritual warfare. By grounding ourselves in the truth of God's Word and relying on the guidance of the Holy Spirit, we can navigate spiritual challenges with wisdom, discernment, and humility. It's only through a sincere pursuit of Biblical illumination that we can engage spiritual warfare effectively and align ourselves with God's divine purposes.

As believers, we have been entrusted with a measure of regional spiritual authority — a divine mandate granted by the Lord Himself. This authority is not arbitrary but is bestowed upon us in accordance with our obedience, faithfulness, and wholehearted commitment to surrendering to the rule and reign of Christ within the confines of our own lives.

Our spiritual authority is linked to our willingness to yield to the lordship of Christ, allowing His divine sovereignty to permeate every aspect of our being. It is rooted in our obedience to His Word, our steadfast faith in His promises, and our unwavering commitment to His kingdom purposes.

This regional spiritual authority extends beyond the boundaries of our individual lives, encompassing the spheres of influence and territories entrusted to us by the Lord. It is a divine commission to advance His kingdom, to proclaim His truth, and to demonstrate His love and power in the world around us.

As stewards of this authority, we are called to exercise it with humility, wisdom, and discernment, recognizing that it is a sacred trust bestowed upon us by the Lord Himself. It is not a license for self-promotion but rather a solemn responsibility to steward the spiritual resources and gifts entrusted to us for the glory of God and the advancement of His kingdom purposes.

> *2 Corinthians 10:13-18 (ESV) But we will not boast beyond limits, but will boast only with regard to the area of influence God assigned to us, to reach even to you. 14 For we are not overextending ourselves, as though we did not reach you. For we were the first to come all the way to you with the gospel of Christ. 15 We do not boast beyond limit in the labors of others. But our hope is that as your faith increases, our area of influence among you may be greatly enlarged, 16 so that we may preach the gospel in lands beyond you, without boasting of work already done in another's area of influence. 17 "Let the one who boasts, boast in the Lord." 18 For it is not the one who commends himself who is approved, but the one whom the Lord commends.*

Possessing Body, Soul, & Spirit As Vessels Of Honor

The foundational principle laid out in the Word of God in 1 Thessalonians 4:4-5 instructs us to prioritize the stewardship of our own bodies, recognizing them as vessels of honor set apart for the service of the Lord. These imperatives underscore the importance of taking a spiritual examination and stewardship, encompassing not only our physical bodies but also our souls and spirits.

To possess our bodies as vessels of honor entails a commitment to aligning every aspect of our being with the will and purposes of God. It involves cultivating a deep awareness of our physical, emotional, and spiritual selves, acknowledging them as sacred instruments through which we can fulfill God's calling and glorify His name.

This process begins with a deliberate pursuit of intimacy with the Lord, allowing His redemptive grace to permeate every dimension of our existence. It involves surrendering our desires, ambitions, and aspirations to His sovereign will, yielding our bodies as living sacrifices holy and acceptable to Him.

> *Romans 12:1-2 (ESV) I appeal to you therefore, brothers, by the mercies of God, to present your bodies as a living sacrifice, holy and acceptable to God, which is your spiritual worship. 2 Do not be conformed to this world, but be transformed by the renewal of your mind, that by testing you may discern what is the will of God, what is good and acceptable and perfect.*

In seeking to possess our bodies, souls, and spirits for the service of the Lord, we embark on a journey of spiritual growth and maturity, characterized by obedience, humility, and steadfast devotion. It is a lifelong pursuit marked by moments of surrender, renewal, and transformation, as we yield to the sanctifying work of the Holy Spirit within us.

Ultimately, as vessels of honor consecrated for divine service, our aim is to reflect the image and likeness of Christ in all that we do, bearing witness to His love, grace, and truth in a world in need of His redeeming presence.

1 Thessalonians 4:4-5 (ESV) that each one of you know how to control his own body in holiness and honor, 5 not in the passion of lust like the Gentiles who do not know God;

What Can I Do To Cancel And Break Demonic Possession Or Oppression?

- *In this type of affliction, there is the need for "deliverance" whereby the afflicted are released from the authority, stronghold, and bondage of demonic activity.*
- *This takes someone who understands spiritual warfare and is willing to take authority over the demonic activity in a person's life.*

Chapter 8
NATURAL LAW OF SIN AND DEATH CAN CAUSE SICKNESS, ILLNESS, DISEASE, AND DEATH

The natural law of sin and death, often referred to as Adam's fall and the sin of rebellion, outlines a fundamental principle governing human existence. This law stems from the Biblical narrative of Adam's transgression, which brought about the pervasive influence of sin and mortality in the world. Consequently, humanity contends with various afflictions such as colds, flu, and other ailments, all symbolic of the relentless grasp of this law. However, the paramount struggle lies in confronting the unstoppable forces of old age and mortality.

The notion that someone as young as ten can succumb to cancer shocks us profoundly, yet we have begrudgingly come to accept it as an inevitable part of existence for individuals nearing eighty. This difference prompts reflection on the acceptance of life's fragility and the inevitability of death. While such acceptance might be deemed commonplace for those separated from a life of faith and redemption, it stands in stark contrast to those who are saved and redeemed.

Within the framework of the law of sin and death, the gradual erosion of humanity and the shortening of life spans across history should warrant our attention.

> *Romans 8:2 (ESV) For the law of the Spirit of life has set you free in Christ Jesus from the law of sin and death.*

The brevity of human life serves as sober reminders of humanity's fallen state and the enduring consequences of Adam's disobedience.

In essence, the natural law of sin and death permeates human existence, manifesting in a multitude of afflictions and ultimately culminating in death. It is a sobering reminder of humanity's inherent vulnerability and the imperative of seeking redemption from the eternal shackles of sin and death through life in our Lord Jesus Christ.

The Span Of Life Under The Law Of Sin And Death:
- *A man at first lived to be almost 1,000 years old.* **(Genesis 5, 9:29)**
- *After the flood, the lifespan was shortened to 500 and 600 years.* **(Genesis 11:10-17)**
- *This was quickly shortened to between 200 and 230 years.* **(Genesis 11:18-23)**
- *Then, the lifespan dropped to between 140 and 205 years.* **(Genesis 11:24-32; 25:7,17; 35:28; 47:28; Job 42:16)**
- *Then, the lifespan dropped to between 110 and 120 years.* **(Genesis 50:26; Deuteronomy 34:7; Joshua 24:29)**
- *Then, the Biblical lifespan dropped to between 80 and 100 years.* **(1 Samuel 4:15; Luke 2:37)**
- *Then, the final Biblical lifespan dropped to between 70 and 80 years.* **(Psalms 90:10)**

Psalms 90:10 (ESV) The years of our life are seventy, or even by reason of strength eighty; yet their span is but toil and trouble; they are soon gone, and we fly away.

BE HEALED

Romans 8:1-3 (ESV) There is therefore now no condemnation for those who are in Christ Jesus. 2 For the law of the Spirit of life has set you free in Christ Jesus from the law of sin and death. 3 For God has done what the law, weakened by the flesh, could not do. By sending his own Son in the likeness of sinful flesh and for sin, he condemned sin in the flesh,

The question arises: why can't Christians experience a progression from "glory to glory"? Why must the journey of a believer be marked by a gradual accumulation of aches and pains as they age, eventually succumbing to affliction and death? Is it not conceivable that a faithful follower of Christ could transition from this earthly existence to the next in ripe old age and robust health? The proposition seems plausible, even promising, and I hold firm to this belief. I am convinced that such occurrences are not merely something we hear about but are destined to become increasingly commonplace.

This optimism stems from a profound shift in the paradigm that governs our existence. No longer are we bound by the constraints of the law of sin and death. Instead, we find ourselves embraced by the liberating embrace of the law of faith and grace. This spiritual shift found in the life of our Lord Jesus Christ and the indwelling Holy Spirit alters our lives, offering the promise of vitality and wholeness.

Under the law of sin and death, humanity was ensnared in a cycle of decay and mortality, with each passing year marked by the relentless onslaught of affliction and decline. However, the advent of the law of faith and grace heralds a new era of possibility and redemption. It offers believers the opportunity to experience life abundantly, liberated from the shackles of sin and its attendant consequences.

In this new covenant in Christ, the forward progress of our lives should no longer be dictated by the inevitability of decay and death. Instead, we are invited to partake in the inexhaustible reservoir of God's grace, which sustains and rejuvenates us even as we journey through the passage of time.

The notion of departing from this world in ripe old age and radiant health is not a mere fantasy but a tangible manifestation of the transformative and redemptive power of the Holy Spirit within us by a life of God's faith and grace. As we continue to embrace the depths of God's love and immerse ourselves in the richness of His grace, we unlock the fullness of our potential as sons and heirs of His kingdom.

Transition from "glory to glory" is not only conceivable but within reach by faith for every believer. By embracing the law of faith and grace, we transcend the limitations of the old order and step into a realm where vitality, wholeness, and divine abundance abound. Let us therefore journey forth with faith and anticipation, confident in the promise life in our Lord Jesus Christ.

What Can We Do?

Even though a Christian is saved by the grace of God, it doesn't automatically imply that they consistently walk and operate under the law of grace in their daily lives. This distinction becomes apparent in our natural activities. For instance, when faced with a headache, our immediate response typically involves reaching for an aspirin rather than turning to prayer and faith for healing. This instinct to rely on conventional remedies reflects a tendency to operate within the framework of the law of sin and death.

BE HEALED

In contrast, responding to challenges with supernatural faith requires a conscious shift towards reliance on the law of the Spirit of life. Rather than defaulting to earthly solutions, believers are called to prioritize seeking the Lord first, trusting in His power to heal and provide solutions to their afflictions, no matter how trivial they may seem.

Embracing the law of the Spirit of life entails a daily commitment to surrendering every aspect of our lives to God's guidance and provision. It means acknowledging His sovereignty over our health, circumstances, and well-being, and approaching each challenge with unwavering faith in the Father's ability to intervene in the name of Jesus and in the power of the Holy Spirit.

Continuing to operate under the law of sin and death perpetuates a cycle of bondage and suffering, wherein afflictions and ailments dominate our existence. This path leads to a life marked by limitations and hardships, wherein the promise of abundant life remains unfulfilled.

In contrast, embracing the law of the Spirit of life opens the door to a life characterized by divine abundance, wherein *every trial becomes an opportunity* for God to demonstrate His faithfulness and provision. By entrusting our lives to His care and guidance, we transcend the constraints of the law and experience the fullness of His grace and power.

While the allure of earthly solutions may be tempting, true freedom and abundance are found in embracing the law of the Spirit of life. By committing ourselves to a lifestyle of faith and surrender, we invite God to work miracles in every aspect of our lives, transforming even the smallest challenges into opportunities for His glory.

It's essential to come to terms with the reality that death is an inevitable part of the human experience. Unless the Lord returns before then, each of us will ultimately face mortality. However, this acknowledgment shouldn't lead us to resign ourselves to a fate of decline and debilitation as we age. Rather, we must vigilantly safeguard our confessions and beliefs, particularly as we advance in years, refusing to align ourselves with the pervasive influence of the law of sin and death.

As we grow older, our words and beliefs carry profound significance. It's crucial that we remain vigilant about the declarations we make concerning our health and vitality. Instead of succumbing to the prevailing stories of decay and deterioration, we must boldly affirm our faith in God's promises of strength, healing, and restoration.

By refusing to yield to the dictates of the law of sin and death, we position ourselves to experience the power of God's grace and provision in our lives. Rather than resigning ourselves to a fate of decline, we can embrace a future marked by vitality, wholeness, and divine abundance.

As stated in Chapter 5, our words carry the authority of life, death, blessings, and cursing. Our confession plays a pivotal role in shaping our reality as we age. By aligning our words and beliefs with the promises of God, we lay the foundation for a future characterized by strength, resilience, and spiritual flourishing. We must be good stewards of our confessions.

As we journey through the passages of time and grow older, the words we speak and the beliefs we hold assume a profound significance. They serve as guiding forces that shape our perception of reality and influence the outcomes we experience. In the face of the prevailing narrative of decay and decline that often accompanies aging, it becomes paramount for us to exercise vigilance over the declarations we make regarding our health and vitality.

Rather than passively accepting the inevitability of physical deterioration, we are called to boldly affirm our faith in the promises of God. Amidst the challenges and uncertainties of aging, we have the opportunity to anchor our hope in the assurance of His strength, healing, and restoration. This affirmation is not merely a verbal exercise but a conscious alignment of our hearts and minds with the eternal truths found in His Word. In Christ we have victory. In Christ we have life.

We have heard the phrase, "give feet to your faith." Our words serve as vehicles through which we manifest our beliefs and shape our reality. As we cultivate a mindset of faith and resilience, we create a fertile ground for God's miraculous intervention to manifest in our lives. With each declaration of His promises, we reinforce our conviction that He is the ultimate source of strength and restoration, capable of breathing new life into even the most weary and worn-down souls. We need to be an obedient people and then like Caleb we must make our confession of faith. He spoke these words of testimony at 85 years old.

> *Numbers 14:24 (ESV) But my servant Caleb, because he has a different spirit and has followed me fully, I will bring into the land into which he went, and his descendants shall possess it.*
>
> *Joshua 14:7-12 (ESV) I was forty years old when Moses the servant of the LORD sent me from Kadesh-barnea to spy out the land, and I brought him word again as it was in my heart. 8 But my brothers who went up with me made the heart of the people melt; yet I wholly followed the LORD my God. 9 And*

Moses swore on that day, saying, 'Surely the land on which your foot has trodden shall be an inheritance for you and your children forever, because you have wholly followed the LORD my God.' 10 And now, behold, the LORD has kept me alive, just as he said, these forty-five years since the time that the LORD spoke this word to Moses, while Israel walked in the wilderness. And now, behold, I am this day eighty-five years old. 11 I am still as strong today as I was in the day that Moses sent me; my strength now is as my strength was then, for war and for going and coming. 12 So now give me this hill country of which the LORD spoke on that day, for you heard on that day how the Anakim were there, with great fortified cities. It may be that the LORD will be with me, and I shall drive them out just as the LORD said."

As believers, it's crucial that we engage in daily confession, affirming our status as individuals no longer bound by the law of sin and death but now governed by the law of the Spirit. The Apostle Paul's admonishment of the Galatians highlights the peril of initially embracing the law of the Spirit, characterized by faith, only to regress back into the grip of the law of sin and death, which is rooted in the flesh.

Our daily confession serves as a powerful reminder of our new identity in Christ and our freedom from the bondage of sin and its consequences. By declaring our allegiance to the law of the Spirit, we reaffirm our reliance on God's grace and the transformative work of His Spirit within us.

Our daily confession acts as a spiritual anchor, guiding us along the path of righteousness and truth. As we declare our identity as people of the Spirit, we fortify our resolve to live lives marked by faith, obedience, and spiritual vitality. May our confession echo the deep conviction of our hearts, as we continually yield to the leading of the Holy Spirit and embrace the abundant life offered to us through Christ Jesus.

Therefore, let us approach the journey of aging with unwavering faith and hope, knowing that in God's unfailing love, there exists the promise of renewal and rejuvenation. As we boldly proclaim His truths over our lives, we stand as living testimonies to His power to transform, heal, and restore, even in the face of the inevitable passage of time.

> *Galatians 3:1-5 (ESV) O foolish Galatians! Who has bewitched you? It was before your eyes that Jesus Christ was publicly portrayed as crucified. 2 Let me ask you only this: Did you receive the Spirit by works of the law or by hearing with faith? 3 Are you so foolish? Having begun by the Spirit, are you now being perfected by the flesh? 4 Did you suffer so many things in vain—if indeed it was in vain? 5 Does he who supplies the Spirit to you and works miracles among you do so by works of the law, or by hearing with faith—*

It is imperative that we embrace truths that promote the well-being of our joints and organs, as recommended in the Bible. This includes cultivating the joy of the Lord and embracing laughter as integral aspects of our lives. By staying attuned to the Lord's guidance, we allow Him to discern the appropriate time for our departure from this earthly existence. In doing so, we ensure that our bodies do not kill us to illness or decay; rather, we surrender our spirits in a manner akin to Jesus, Stephen, and Paul.

For those of us who embarked on this journey of faith under the law of the Spirit, it is essential to remain steadfast in our commitment. We must not regress into bondage under the law of sin and death, relinquishing control of our bodies, souls, and spirits. Instead, we are called to walk in faith, continually yielding to the transformative power of the Spirit.

By maintaining our fellowship with the Lord Jesus Christ and abiding in His truth, we safeguard our physical and spiritual well-being. Let us persevere in our faith journey, anchored in the promises of God, and empowered by the law of the Spirit. In doing so, we experience the fullness of life and walk in alignment with His divine purpose for us.

What Can I Do To Cancel And Break The Hold Of The Natural Law Of Sin And Death?

- *Stay in a place of confessing the Word instead of confessing the ailment, symptom, disease, or affliction.*
- *Stay in a place of faith by believing that divine health is what God desires for us to be for His glory.*

Run the course and keep the faith. Finish well.

Let's recap the first six causes of sickness, illness, disease, and death.

1. *Personal Sins Can Cause Sickness, Illness, Disease. And Death.*
2. *Sins Of The Forefathers Can Cause Sickness, Illness, Disease And Death.*

3. *Word Curses Can Cause Sickness, Illness, Disease, And Death.*
4. *Ungodly Soul Ties Can Cause Sickness, Illness, Disease, And Death.*
5. *Demonic Presence In Way Of Oppression Or Possession Can Cause Sickness, Illness, Disease, And Death.*
6. *Natural Law Of Sin And Death Can Cause Sickness, Illness, Disease And Death.*

Chapter 9
SICKNESS, ILLNESS, DISEASE, AND DEATH CAN COME UPON US FOR GOD'S GLORY TO BE MANIFESTED

Supernatural healing is also manifested for the glory of God. It represents God revealing His presence in tangible ways. Consider the narrative in John 9, where a blind man becomes the focal point of discussion among the disciples. They inquire whether the man's blindness was a result of his own sin or that of his parents. Jesus responds, rebuking their limited understanding, indicating that their analysis was confined to attributing ailments solely to human sin or demonic influence.

> *John 9:1-7 (ESV) As he passed by, he saw a man blind from birth. 2 And his disciples asked him, "Rabbi, who sinned, this man or his parents, that he was born blind?" 3 Jesus answered, "It was not that this man sinned, or his parents, but that the works of God might be displayed in him. 4 We must work the works of him who sent me while it is day; night is coming, when no one can work. 5 As long as I am in the world, I am the light of the world." 6 Having said these things, he spit on the ground and made mud with the saliva. Then he anointed the man's eyes with the mud 7 and said to him, "Go, wash in the pool of Siloam" (which means Sent). So he went and washed and came back seeing.*

BE HEALED

In the passage found in John 9:1-7, Jesus clarifies that the blindness afflicting the man and whether his parents were sinless or not was not the issue at hand. His response does not negate the concept of generational sins leading to sickness, disease, and affliction, nor does it dismiss the idea of personal sins causing illness and suffering. Rather, Jesus explicitly denies that either of these reasons were the cause of this man's blindness.

This particular man's blindness, according to Jesus, served a singular purpose: to provide an opportunity for the works and glory of God the Father to be revealed and manifested. In other words, the man's condition was not a punishment for sin, but rather an opportunity through which God could demonstrate His power and bring glory to Himself. Jesus's words emphasize the deeper spiritual significance behind the man's affliction, highlighting God's sovereignty and His ability to use even suffering for His divine purposes.

God allowed the blindness of this man as a means through which the Father's glory could be revealed in the eventual healing. It's a crucial point often overlooked: God's glory wasn't magnified by how adeptly the blind man navigated society despite his impairment or how he managed to acquire a trade despite his affliction. Rather, the true glorification of God occurred solely through the miraculous healing of the man's blindness.

It's important to note that the text doesn't suggest God directly inflicted the blindness upon him, but rather it was allowed to occur within the divine plan. There came a specific time when God's magnificence was to be showcased, and the only manner in which God's grandeur was truly exalted in connection to the man's blindness was through his complete and total healing. This highlights the divine orchestration behind the man's affliction and subsequent restoration, underscoring God's sovereignty and His ultimate purpose in glorifying Himself through the restoration of the blind man's sight.

What Can We Do?

It is imperative that we personally seek the Lord, both for ourselves and for those we intend to pray for, regarding the underlying causes of our ailments and sicknesses. The Father's desire is to be exalted and glorified through the process of healing. He longs for those who may not yet know Him to come to a position of faith in Him as a result of experiencing healing.

Similar to the disciples' misunderstanding in the Biblical narrative, we too may misinterpret the root cause of some sicknesses. Therefore, it is essential for us to operate with the gifts of knowledge and discernment, seeking insight from the Holy Spirit to discern whether an illness is intended as an opportunity for healing that glorifies the Father. Through prayer and spiritual discernment, we can align ourselves with God's will and participate in His work of healing and restoration, ultimately bringing glory to His name.

Chapter 10
JUDGMENT OF THE FLESH FOR THE PURPOSE OF RECONCILIATION CAN CAUSE SICKNESS, ILLNESS, DISEASE, AND DEATH

God uses judgment and reconciliation, a process often referred to as the "buffeting of the flesh," to draw individuals back to His heart and to serve as a chastisement for those who persist in their refusal to repent. In this context, the concept involves allowing someone's flesh to be subjected to trials and tribulations, even at the hands of the enemy, with the ultimate goal of saving their soul.

The underlying idea is profound: would one prefer to see a loved one lead a seemingly healthy life on earth only to face eternal damnation in hell, or endure a life marked by physical afflictions and challenges here while securing eternal life? This approach isn't solely about judgment; rather, it's a mechanism for reconciling individuals with God.

Many individuals fail to recognize the need for God or spiritual matters because they prioritize themselves and their physical well-being above all else. By allowing hardships and ailments to enter their lives, God strips away the idolatry of health and self-worship, creating an opportunity for them to recognize the necessity of seeking our Lord Jesus Christ. Through this process of buffeting, God seeks to realign priorities, leading individuals towards a deeper understanding of His grace, mercy, and eternal salvation.

1 Timothy 1:18-20 (ESV) This charge I entrust to you, Timothy, my child, in accordance with the prophecies previously made about you, that by them you may wage the good warfare, 19 holding faith and a good conscience. By rejecting this, some have made shipwreck of their faith, 20 among whom are Hymenaeus and Alexander, whom I have handed over to Satan that they may learn not to blaspheme.

2 Timothy 4:14-15 (ESV) Alexander the coppersmith did me great harm; the Lord will repay him according to his deeds. 15 Beware of him yourself, for he strongly opposed our message.

2 Timothy 2:16-17 (ESV) But avoid irreverent babble, for it will lead people into more and more ungodliness, 17 and their talk will spread like gangrene. Among them are Hymenaeus and Philetus,

At times, individuals find themselves elevated to positions of authority or esteem that surpass what is appropriate for them. In such instances, they may encounter challenges or setbacks in their physical experiences, serving as visible reminders to others that their elevated status is unwarranted. This phenomenon is colloquially expressed as "that person has been cut down to size."

Consider the Apostle Paul as a case in point. Some individuals elevated him to a status far beyond that of an ordinary man, even going so far as to regard him as equal to our Lord, essentially deifying him. This elevation of Paul beyond his rightful human status illustrates how people can exalt individuals beyond reasonable bounds, leading to distortions in perception and belief.

The impact of Paul's teachings led some who had initially followed John the Baptist and later embraced the teachings of Jesus Christ to shift their focus toward Paul as the primary figure to emulate and even worship. This shift highlights the powerful sway Paul held over the hearts and minds of those who sought spiritual guidance and leadership during his time.

Paul, through his remarkable revelations regarding matters of the Kingdom, ignited a sense of awe and admiration among certain believers, fostering a perception akin to that of a Superman or hero figure. In a vision, the Father elevated Paul into His presence, unveiling profound insights that Paul later revealed in fourteen significant books under the guidance of the Holy Spirit. As Paul poured out the heart of the Father through his writings, his influence grew exponentially.

The Father permitted Paul to undergo trials and challenges in his physical body, serving as a reminder to both Paul himself and those who followed him that he was simply a mortal man, subject to human frailties and limitations. This allowance by the Father was intended to prevent Paul from being idolized or worshipped by his followers.

Through the experiences of hardship and adversity that Paul faced, the Father sought to instill humility and a sense of humanity in both Paul and his followers. It was a moving lesson that even someone as influential and spiritually attuned as Paul remained fallible and susceptible to the struggles inherent in the human condition. This reminder helped to maintain the proper perspective on Paul's role and significance within the context of his followers' spiritual journey, ensuring that their reverence remained directed towards the Lord Jesus Christ rather than towards a mortal being.

1 Corinthians 5:1-5 (ESV) It is actually reported that there is sexual immorality among you, and of a kind that is not tolerated even among pagans, for a man has his father's wife. 2 And you are arrogant! Ought you not rather to mourn? Let him who has done this be removed from among you. 3 For though absent in body, I am present in spirit; and as if present, I have already pronounced judgment on the one who did such a thing. 4 When you are assembled in the name of the Lord Jesus and my spirit is present, with the power of our Lord Jesus, 5 you are to deliver this man to Satan for the destruction of the flesh, so that his spirit may be saved in the day of the Lord.

2 Corinthians 12:7-10 (ESV) So to keep me from becoming conceited because of the surpassing greatness of the revelations, a thorn was given me in the flesh, a messenger of Satan to harass me, to keep me from becoming conceited. 8 Three times I pleaded with the Lord about this, that it should leave me. 9 But he said to me, "My grace is sufficient for you, for my power is made perfect in weakness." Therefore I will boast all the more gladly of my weaknesses, so that the power of Christ may rest upon me. 10 For the sake of Christ, then, I am content with weaknesses, insults, hardships, persecutions, and calamities. For when I am weak, then I am strong.

Once more, it's important to emphasize that the Father permitted trials, tribulations, and afflictions to befall Paul, not to diminish him, but to underscore to others that Paul was neither the Messiah nor divine. This served as a profound lesson against the sin of idolatry.

BE HEALED

Through Paul's struggles and challenges, the Father intended to impart a clear message: that true devotion should be reserved for God alone. By allowing Paul to face hardships, the Father demonstrated the danger of elevating mortal beings to the status of idols or deities, reminding believers of the imperative to keep their worship focused solely on the Father. This teaching was a powerful deterrent against the temptation to idolize human figures, reaffirming the supremacy of God in the hearts and minds of believers.

Paul's Thorn In The Flesh:

The inquiry into Paul's "thorn in the flesh" prompts a deeper exploration of its meaning and significance. While some teachings suggest that Paul's deteriorating eyesight was the source of his affliction, such an interpretation might oversimplify the matter. Although evidence suggests Paul struggled with poor eyesight, reducing his thorn in the flesh to a physical ailment such as failing eyesight would oversimplify the complexity of his experience.

To glean a more comprehensive understanding, it is imperative to examine the context provided in 2 Corinthians 11 and 12. These passages offer insights into Paul's perspective on his affliction and its broader implications. Paul's acknowledgment of his thorn in the flesh underscores his awareness that it was not a personal judgment but a corrective measure directed towards those within the body of Christ who sought to elevate him to a status equal to that of the Lord Jesus Christ.

Paul's thorn in the flesh served as a reminder of the dangers of idolatry and the importance of maintaining a proper reverence for God. By grappling with this affliction, Paul confronted the temptation for believers to exalt mortal beings to divine status, emphasizing the need for humility and spiritual discernment within the Christian community.

Thus, delving into the context of Paul's writings offers a more refined and exact understanding of his thorn in the flesh, highlighting its symbolic significance and its role in addressing broader theological themes within the early Christian movement.

It's crucial to grasp that Paul perceived the affliction upon his flesh not as a personal indictment, but rather as a corrective measure aimed at those within the body of Christ who sought to elevate him to a status comparable to that of the Lord Jesus Christ. This perspective underscores Paul's profound understanding of the dynamics within the Christian community and his commitment to upholding the primacy of Christ.

Paul's recognition that the judgment on his flesh was not directed at him personally reflects his humility and spiritual discernment. He discerned the danger of being exalted to a divine level, recognizing the inherent risk of idolatry and the distortion of the fundamental tenets of the Christian faith.

> *2 Corinthians 11:22-33 (ESV) Are they Hebrews? So am I. Are they Israelites? So am I. Are they offspring of Abraham? So am I. 23 Are they servants of Christ? I am a better one—I am talking like a madman—with far greater labors, far more imprisonments, with countless beatings, and often near death. 24 Five times I received at the hands of the Jews the forty lashes less one. 25 Three times I was beaten with rods. Once I was stoned. Three times I was shipwrecked; a night and a day I was adrift at sea; 26 on frequent journeys, in danger from rivers, danger from robbers, danger from my own people, danger*

from Gentiles, danger in the city, danger in the wilderness, danger at sea, danger from false brothers; 27 in toil and hardship, through many a sleepless night, in hunger and thirst, often without food, in cold and exposure. 28 And, apart from other things, there is the daily pressure on me of my anxiety for all the churches. 29 Who is weak, and I am not weak? Who is made to fall, and I am not indignant? 30 If I must boast, I will boast of the things that show my weakness. 31 The God and Father of the Lord Jesus, he who is blessed forever, knows that I am not lying. 32 At Damascus, the governor under King Aretas was guarding the city of Damascus in order to seize me, 33 but I was let down in a basket through a window in the wall and escaped his hands.

In 2 Corinthians 11:22-33, Paul provides a detailed account of the numerous challenges, adversities, and sufferings he endured throughout his ministry. Delving into Paul's catalog of afflictions offers profound insights into the depth and breadth of his experiences, revealing that his thorn in the flesh far exceeded mere physical ailments, such as failing eyesight.

Paul's listing of his afflictions serves as a witness to the intensity of his dedication to spreading the gospel and advancing the cause of Christ. From beatings and imprisonments to shipwrecks and dangers from various sources, Paul's life was marked by a continuous cycle of trials and tribulations. His relentless commitment to proclaiming the message of salvation amidst persecution and adversity underscores his unwavering faith and resilience in the face of hardship.

By chronicling his sufferings in such detail, Paul offers a glimpse into the profound challenges he confronted as a servant of Christ. Paul's willingness to share his struggles with the Corinthian congregation demonstrates his vulnerability and authenticity as a spiritual leader, inspiring others to persevere in their faith journey despite the trials they may encounter.

In essence, Paul's list of afflictions serves as sober reminder of the reality of suffering in the Christian life and the transformative power of God's grace amidst adversity. It invites believers to embrace their own struggles with courage and faith, trusting in God's provision and steadfast love to sustain them through every trial and tribulation.

- *Frequently imprisoned*
- *Faced the valley of the shadow of death, often*
- *Whipped five times with 39 stripes*
- *Beaten with rods three times*
- *Stoned and left for dead once*
- *Shipwrecked three times*
- *Thrown into a deep dungeon*
- *Faced rough waters on the sea*
- *Faced robbers*
- *His friends turned violently against him*
- *Lost heathen turned violently against him*
- *He faced constant danger for his life both in the city, in the country, and on the seas*
- *False believers set themselves against him*
- *He was often tired, going without rest*
- *He was often in pain from his violent trials and tribulations*
- *He was always looking over his shoulder, watching to see if someone was trying to kill him*
- *He spent a lot of time hungry and thirsty*
- *He was called to fast often*

- He was underdressed for the weather situation, leaving him cold
- Then, his constant care for the welfare of the churches

2 Corinthians 12:1-6 (ESV) I must go on boasting. Though there is nothing to be gained by it, I will go on to visions and revelations of the Lord. 2 I know a man in Christ who fourteen years ago was caught up to the third heaven—whether in the body or out of the body I do not know, God knows. 3 And I know that this man was caught up into paradise—whether in the body or out of the body I do not know, God knows— 4 and he heard things that cannot be told, which man may not utter. 5 On behalf of this man I will boast, but on my own behalf I will not boast, except of my weaknesses— 6 though if I should wish to boast, I would not be a fool, for I would be speaking the truth; but I refrain from it, so that no one may think more of me than he sees in me or hears from me.

What Can We Do?

I have encountered situations where individuals have requested me to pray for the spiritual redemption of their loved ones, even if it means subjecting them to turning them over to be enemy so they would be buffeted in the flesh. This means they would suffer physical suffering. This request delves deep into the complexities of faith and the nature of God's intervention.

When someone asks us to pray for a loved one to undergo trials in the flesh for the sake of their spiritual salvation, it demands a profound understanding of what such a prayer entails. It's not a casual request; it's a plea to intervene in the between physical and spiritual realms. We must grasp the gravity of our words and actions, fully cognizant of the potential ramifications. We must know what we are praying for here and be willing to pay the cost.

Consider a scenario where a loved one suffers a stroke as a result of such a prayer. We then find ourselves obligated to provide round-the-clock care for them for the remainder of their lives. This is not a burden to be taken lightly. It's a commitment that could alter the direction and destiny of our own lives, binding us to the consequences of our supplications.

In such moments, it's crucial to discern whether our prayers align with the will of the Father. Are we truly hearing the voice of the Father in our prayers, or are we acting out of our own emotions, be it hurt, anger, or a desire for retribution? It's a question that demands a deep self-examination and honesty.

We must examine our hearts meticulously, ensuring that our motivations are pure, and our intentions are guided by love and compassion rather than by personal grievances or a desire to manipulate God. Know this. God cannot tempt us, and He cannot be tempted. He cannot be manipulated to do something outside of His will and character. Praying for the spiritual well-being of others should stem from a place of genuine concern and goodwill, devoid of ulterior motives or hidden agendas.

Ultimately, when we offer prayers of this nature, we must be prepared to accept the consequences, whatever they may be. It's a solemn pact with the divine, a recognition of our role as intermediaries between the physical and spiritual realms. In the end, it's not just about the words we utter or the prayers we offer, but the sincerity and depth of our commitment to the greater good for the glory of God.

Chapter 11
TAKING THE LORD'S SUPPER IN AN UNWORTHY MANNER CAN CAUSE SICKNESS, ILLNESS, DISEASE, AND DEATH

In 1 Corinthians 11:23-27, the apostle Paul emphasizes the command for believers to partake in the Lord's Supper collectively, emphasizing its significance within the community of faith. This sacred practice, unfortunately, often falls prey to misuse, abuse, and trivialization among many who profess to follow Christ. It is a sober reality that while Scripture offers guidance and instruction on various aspects of Christian living, few passages carry as grave a warning as the one regarding the Lord's Supper.

Within verse 27 of this passage, Paul issues a solemn caution against partaking in the Lord's Supper in an unworthy manner. This admonition serves as a stark reminder of the reverence and discernment required when participating in this sacred ritual. The gravity of the warning emphasizes the importance of approaching the Lord's Table with humility, sincerity, and a clear conscience.

The Lord's Supper, instituted by Jesus Himself during the Last Supper with His disciples, holds profound spiritual significance for believers. It serves as a tangible expression of Christ's sacrificial love, symbolizing His body broken and His blood shed for the redemption of humanity. As such, partaking in the Lord's Supper is not merely a ritualistic observance but a solemn act of remembrance, gratitude, and communion with God and fellow believers.

To partake in the Lord's Supper in an unworthy manner is to trivialize its sacredness and disregard its profound implications. Such irreverence not only dishonors the sacrifice of Christ but also invites God's judgment upon oneself. Therefore, believers are urged to approach the Lord's Table with utmost reverence, examining their hearts and motives before participating.

The warning articulated in 1 Corinthians 11:27 serves as a sobering reminder of the significance of the Lord's Supper within the life of the church. It compels believers to approach this sacred ordinance with humility, reverence, and genuine repentance, mindful of its profound implications for their spiritual journey as the body of Christ.

> *1 Corinthians 11:23-27 (ESV) For I received from the Lord what I also delivered to you, that the Lord Jesus on the night when he was betrayed took bread, 24 and when he had given thanks, he broke it, and said, "This is my body, which is for you. Do this in remembrance of me." 25 In the same way also he took the cup, after supper, saying, "This cup is the new covenant in my blood. Do this, as often as you drink it, in remembrance of me." 26 For as often as you eat this bread and drink the cup, you proclaim the Lord's death until he comes. 27 Whoever, therefore, eats the bread or drinks the cup of the Lord in an unworthy manner* **will be guilty concerning the body and blood of the Lord.**

In the passage found in 1 Corinthians 11:28-32, the apostle Paul delivers a solemn warning regarding the consequences of partaking in the Lord's Supper in an unworthy manner. This warning extends beyond mere spiritual implications; it reveals the possibility of experiencing physical judgment, manifesting as weakness, sickness, or even death. The gravity of this admonition underscores the seriousness with which believers should approach the Lord's Table.

Paul emphasizes the necessity for each individual to engage in rigorous self-examination before participating in the Lord's Supper. This spiritual process is crucial to discerning one's spiritual state and ensuring that one approaches the sacred ordinance with sincerity and reverence.

Paul highlights that through conscientious self-judgment, believers can avoid being judged by the Lord. Neglecting the imperative of self-examination and failing to address our spiritual deficiencies leave us vulnerable to the judgment of the Lord.

This "hard saying" of verse 32 emphasizes the profound implications of God's judgment and the urgency of heeding Paul's warning regarding the Lord's Supper. It beckons believers to delve deeper into the complexities of the Father's justice, mercy, and human responsibility in the context of Christian faith and practice.

In essence, the warning articulated in 1 Corinthians 11:28-32 serves as a reminder of the significance of the Lord's Supper within the life of the church. It emphasizes the imperative of personal accountability, spiritual discernment, and sincere repentance as integral components of faithful discipleship. Thus, believers are encouraged to approach the Lord's Table with humility, reverence, and unwavering devotion, mindful of the weighty implications of their participation in this sacred ordinance.

> *1 Corinthians 11:28-32 (ESV) Let a person examine himself, then, and so eat of the bread and drink of the cup. 29 For anyone who eats and drinks without*

> *discerning the body eats and drinks judgment on himself. 30 That is why many of you are weak and ill, and some have died. 31 But if we judged ourselves truly, we would not be judged. 32 But when we are judged by the Lord, we are disciplined so that we may not be condemned along with the world.*

In 1 Corinthians 11:30-32, the Apostle Paul addresses the repercussions of misbehavior during the observance of the Lord's Supper. Paul had cautioned the Corinthians about partaking in the Lord's Supper in an unworthy manner. Interpreting what constitutes celebrating the Lord's table unworthily can vary among different perspectives. However, the prevalent understanding is that Paul referred to being in a state of sin.

The sins highlighted within the Corinthian church encompassed division and jealousy among its members. Additionally, disorder marred the observance of the Lord's Supper, accompanied by a failure to demonstrate love and generosity towards the less fortunate by the affluent members, as well as instances of gluttony and drunkenness. The sinful condition of this church community is readily apparent.

Partaking in the Lord's Supper while the church remains divided constitutes a sin against the unity of Christ's body. Due to the continuation of these sins, many among the community have become physically weak, sick, and some have even died. A more accurate rendering would suggest that this is why a considerable number among you are experiencing weakness, illness, and the unfortunate outcome of death.

We need to perceive this illness and death from a spiritual perspective. Their actions transgressed a spiritual principle, leading to a spiritual judgment that manifested in physical ailments and death.

As the Lord's Supper has evolved into a routine ritual, many just view it loosely as an observance to commemorate the death, burial, and resurrection of the Lord. However, the church has neglected the caution against participating while engulfed in personal or collective sin. The act of partaking in the Lord's Supper serves as a discerning judgment, revealing the concealed sins of the heart.

What Can We Do?

We must earnestly examine ourselves and ensure reconciliation with God and fellow members of our church community are in order before sharing bread together.

When we partake in the Lord's Supper, we embark on a journey through time, encompassing the past, present, and future in a single glorious act. We reflect back to the dawn of humanity, witnessing the entry of sin into the world through the fall of man. Our gaze then shifts to an event 2,000 years ago, when our Lord's body was broken, and His blood was shed for our redemption, bridging the gap between humanity and God. Furthermore, we anticipate the future reign of our imminent King, who will establish His kingdom on earth, where we will walk eternally with Him. However, most importantly, we examine our present lives, assessing our standing in relationship and fellowship with God the Father.

We should refrain from partaking in the Lord's Supper if we harbor uncertainty about our salvation. Similarly, if we find ourselves entangled in sin through our words, actions, or thoughts, we should abstain from participating. Moreover, the Lord's Supper ought not to be treated as a mere meal; rather, it should be a solemn recognition of God's grace in offering His Son as a sacrifice for our sins. Therefore, prior to partaking in the Lord's Supper, the Scriptures advise us to thoroughly examine ourselves.

Prayer:

Father, we humbly ask to come before Your table with clean hands and pure hearts. As we acknowledge the profound sacrifice of the cross, we openly admit our collective sinfulness and unworthiness. Please forgive us in Jesus' name for harboring contentious and divisive attitudes in our hearts. Forgive us for yielding to the desires and deeds of the flesh. Grant us the grace to approach the Lord's Supper in the Spirit, fostering peace with all individuals. We ask this in the name of our Lord and Savior, Jesus Christ.

Chapter 12
LYING TO THE HOLY SPIRIT CAN CAUSE SICKNESS, ILLNESS, DISEASE, AND DEATH

Lying to the Holy Spirit has not proven to be a healthy occupation within the Scriptures. Such deceit led to the demise of two individuals who were evidently involved in the fellowship. The narrative of Ananias and Sapphira vividly illustrates this consequence. Allow me to recount their story.

Based on the accounts provided in Acts 4:34-37 and 5:1-11, it appears that the leadership of the early Christian community was familiar with Ananias and Sapphira. Moreover, it suggests that Ananias and Sapphira were aware of the church community plans to distribute their possessions among fellow believers.

In Acts 4:34-37, we learn about the generosity of the early believers, who sold their possessions and shared the proceeds with those in need. Although we cannot argue from Biblical silence, Ananias and Sapphira were seemingly part of this community, witnessing the selfless acts of giving.

> *Acts 4:34-37 (ESV) There was not a needy person among them, for as many as were owners of lands or houses sold them and brought the proceeds of what was sold 35 and laid it at the apostles' feet, and it was distributed to each as any had need. 36 Thus Joseph, who was also called by the apostles Barnabas (which means son of encouragement), a Levite, a native of Cyprus, 37 sold a field that belonged to him and brought the money and laid it at the apostles' feet.*

However, in Acts 5:1-11, we encounter the unfortunate account of Ananias and Sapphira's deceit. They conspired to keep a portion of the proceeds from the sale of their property for themselves while pretending to give the entire amount to the apostles. This deception led to their tragic demise as they fell dead before the apostle Peter.

The fact that the apostles were aware of Ananias and Sapphira's names and actions suggests a level of familiarity and perhaps involvement within the church community. Their attempt to deceive highlights the severity of their actions and serves as a warning within the early Christian fellowship and for us today.

The possessions they owned were under their control, allowing them the freedom to decide how to use them. They made the choice to sell their land and entrusted the proceeds to Peter for distribution as needs arose.

Acts 5:1 (ESV) But a man named Ananias, with his wife Sapphira, sold a piece of property,

In Acts 5:1-4, we encounter the story of Ananias and Sapphira, who sold a piece of property. However, it seems that the value of the land was considerable, prompting Ananias and Sapphira to conspire to withhold a portion of the proceeds for themselves. Interestingly, the act of keeping part of the money from the sale wasn't what ultimately led to their deaths.

As Peter later clarified, the land was indeed their property, and even after its sale, the money rightfully belonged to them. The issue at hand wasn't about whether they were obliged to give all the proceeds from the sale. Instead, it was about their deceitful intentions and their attempt to deceive the church family and God Himself by pretending to offer the entire sum while secretly keeping back a portion for themselves.

> Acts 5:2-4 (ESV) and with his wife's knowledge he kept back for himself some of the proceeds and brought only a part of it and laid it at the apostles' feet. 3 But Peter said, "Ananias, why has Satan filled your heart to lie to the Holy Spirit and to keep back for yourself part of the proceeds of the land? 4 While it remained unsold, did it not remain your own? And after it was sold, was it not at your disposal? Why is it that you have contrived this deed in your heart? You have not lied to man but to God."

As detailed in Acts 5:4-10, the critical moment arose when Ananias and Sapphira chose to deceive by falsely claiming that they were presenting the full 100% of the proceeds from the sale of their property to the Apostles. Peter emphasized that their deception wasn't merely directed towards him or the leadership of the church but constituted a deceitful act against the Holy Spirit and God Himself.

Following Ananias's demise, Sapphira entered the scene and continued the lie her husband had initiated. Her deception, like his, resulted in immediate judgment as she, too, fell dead upon confronting Peter about the fabricated story. These events emphasize the sanctity of truthfulness and integrity within the fellowship of believers, highlighting the seriousness of lying to the Holy Spirit.

As a consequence, two individuals within the community of Saints lost their lives, instilling a deep reverence for God among the rest of the group. Following Ananias's sudden death due to his deceit before the Holy Spirit, his wife entered the scene and continued the falsehood. However, she met the same fate as her husband, succumbing to death for lying to the Holy Spirit.

> *Acts 5:5-10 (ESV) When Ananias heard these words, he fell down and breathed his last. And great fear came upon all who heard of it. 6 The young men rose and wrapped him up and carried him out and buried him. 7 After an interval of about three hours his wife came in, not knowing what had happened. 8 And Peter said to her, "Tell me whether you sold the land for so much." And she said, "Yes, for so much." 9 But Peter said to her, "How is it that you have agreed together to test the Spirit of the Lord? Behold, the feet of those who have buried your husband are at the door, and they will carry you out." 10 Immediately she fell down at his feet and breathed her last. When the young men came in they found her dead, and they carried her out and buried her beside her husband.*

The consequence of their deceit was severe: both Ananias and Sapphira met untimely deaths within the community of believers. Their deaths served as a stark warning, instilling a profound fear of God among the rest of the congregation.

A profound sense of awe and reverence gripped the believers as they witnessed the immediate judgment that ensued from deceiving the Holy Spirit.

> *Acts 5:11 (ESV) And great fear came upon the whole church and upon all who heard of these things.*

The Old Testament, particularly the book of Proverbs, cautions against boasting about false gifts. Additionally, the prophet Isaiah delivers a message regarding wearying God, which implies testing His patience, causing Him grief, or provoking His disgust with our actions or attitudes.

> Proverbs 25:14 (ESV) Like clouds and wind without rain is a man who boasts of a gift he does not give.

> Isaiah 7:13 (ESV) And he said, "Hear then, O house of David! Is it too little for you to weary men, that you weary my God also?

What Can We Do?

In Ephesians 4:30, 1 Thessalonians 5:19, and 2 Corinthians 9:6-7, the imperative to refrain from grieving or quenching the Holy Spirit emphasizes the significance of our actions and attitudes. The principle of reaping what we sow is stressed, highlighting the importance of sowing generously and with integrity, particularly in the context of sharing our blessings with others.

It's crucial that our giving stems from a sincere and thoughtful decision made in our hearts. We are urged to be transparent and truthful about our intentions, especially when the occasion arises to share what we have been blessed with. This call to honesty and sincerity reflects the deeper spiritual principle of stewardship and generosity, encouraging believers to align their actions with the guidance of the Holy Spirit and the values of integrity and goodwill.

> Ephesians 4:30 (ESV) And do not grieve the Holy Spirit of God, by whom you were sealed for the day of redemption.

> 1 Thessalonians 5:19 (ESV) Do not quench the Spirit.

2 Corinthians 9:6-7 (ESV) The point is this: whoever sows sparingly will also reap sparingly, and whoever sows bountifully will also reap bountifully. 7 Each one must give as he has decided in his heart, not reluctantly or under compulsion, for God loves a cheerful giver.

Chapter 13
UNFORGIVENESS CAN CAUSE SICKNESS, ILLNESS, DISEASE, AND DEATH

Unforgiveness operates like a malignant cancer, cunningly consuming the essence of the soul and poisoning relationships. It's akin to relinquishing control of one's life to someone else, allowing their actions or words to dictate the course of one's existence. It is like permitting someone else to drive the bus of your life.

Proverbs 4 offers profound insights into this matter, guiding us toward wisdom and understanding.

> *Proverbs 4:20-24 (ESV) My son, be attentive to my words; incline your ear to my sayings. 21 Let them not escape from your sight; keep them within your heart. 22 For they are life to those who find them, and healing to all their flesh. 23 Keep your heart with all vigilance, for from it flow the springs of life. 24 Put away from you crooked speech, and put devious talk far from you.*

Proverbs 4:20-24 implores us to heed wisdom with unwavering attention and to internalize its teachings deep within our hearts. The passage emphasizes the life-giving and healing power of wisdom when embraced and lived out faithfully. Verse 23 stands out as an excellent reminder to guard our hearts diligently, for they serve as the wellsprings of life itself. The Hebrew term for "springs" in this context, tosaah, conveys the idea of boundaries or sources from which life flows. Thus, the contents of our hearts dictate the course and quality of our lives, shaping the boundaries of our existence and influencing all that emanates from us. Let me repeat this. What is in our hearts reveals and shapes our lives.

King David, in Psalms 109:2, provides a vivid illustration of the consequences of harboring ill intentions within the heart. He describes a scenario where individuals resort to cursing instead of blessing others, highlighting the detrimental impact of malicious speech on relationships and community dynamics. David identifies those responsible for such actions, urging reflection on the heart's condition and the words it generates.

> *Psalms 109:2 (ESV) For wicked and deceitful mouths are opened against me, speaking against me with lying tongues.*

In Psalms 109:16-19, David illuminates the profound connection between the inner workings of a person's heart and the expressions of their tongue, highlighting how these elements ultimately serve as judges of one's character and actions. In other words. A man's heart and tongue will judge him.

David's verses offer insight into the power of both the heart and the tongue to shape and define a person's life. He illustrates how the evil intentions harbored within the heart inevitably find expression through the words spoken by the tongue. Our Lord Jesus Christ spoke these same thoughts. These words, laden with malice and deceit, become a testimony to the true condition of the heart, serving as indictments against the individual.

> *Matthew 12:34-37 (ESV) You brood of vipers! How can you speak good, when you are evil? For out of*

> the abundance of the heart the mouth speaks. 35 The good person out of his good treasure brings forth good, and the evil person out of his evil treasure brings forth evil. 36 I tell you, on the day of judgment people will give account for every careless word they speak, 37 for by your words you will be justified, and by your words you will be condemned."

David's reflection emphasizes the responsibility each person bears for the thoughts they nurture within their hearts and the words they choose to utter. It serves as a sober reminder of the intimate connection between the inner landscape of the heart and the outward expressions of speech, emphasizing the need for vigilance and mindfulness in both realms.

> Psalms 109:16-20 (ESV) For he did not remember to show kindness, but pursued the poor and needy and the brokenhearted, to put them to death. 17 He loved to curse; let curses come upon him! He did not delight in blessing; may it be far from him! 18 He clothed himself with cursing as his coat; may it soak into his body like water, like oil into his bones! 19 May it be like a garment that he wraps around him, like a belt that he puts on every day! 20 May this be the reward of my accusers from the LORD, of those who speak evil against my life!

Let's face the truth. When we harbor unforgiveness in our hearts, our words will not bring blessings upon those we hold resentment toward. Instead, when we talk about them, our words will likely be laced with curses, reflecting our perspective on the perceived injustices they've inflicted upon us.

David vividly illustrates the consequences of cursing his adversaries in Psalms. He articulates that the act of cursing others ultimately defiles his own body, likening it to the discomfort and swelling akin to water retention and joint pain.

Moreover, in the New Testament, there's a profound warning against harboring bitterness in our lives. This warning places bitterness in the same category as immorality, highlighting its detrimental impact on our spiritual well-being and relationships. The parallel drawn between bitterness and immorality highlights the seriousness with which we should regard the presence of bitterness in our hearts. This urges us to address it with the same urgency and vigilance as other sinful inclinations.

> *Hebrews 12:14-17 (ESV) Strive for peace with everyone, and for the holiness without which no one will see the Lord. 15 See to it that no one fails to obtain the grace of God; that no "root of bitterness" springs up and causes trouble, and by it many become defiled; 16 that no one is sexually immoral or unholy like Esau, who sold his birthright for a single meal. 17 For you know that afterward, when he desired to inherit the blessing, he was rejected, for he found no chance to repent, though he sought it with tears.*
>
> *1 Peter 2:1 (ESV) So put away all malice and all deceit and hypocrisy and envy and all slander.*

Unforgiveness Is A Sin

It's a truth that often escapes many believers: unforgiveness is indeed a sin. God's commandments are clear on this matter; we are called to forgive just as we have been forgiven. The very essence of walking in the love of God mirrors the example set by our Lord Jesus Christ, who forgave even those who wronged Him and serves as our model.

A genuine journey of faith revolves around our ability to extend forgiveness. Our capacity to receive forgiveness from the Father is intricately linked to our willingness to forgive others. This principle is underscored in Mark 11:25, where Jesus instructs us that when we stand in prayer, we must forgive anyone against whom we hold grievances. This act of forgiveness not only aligns us with the heart of the Father but also opens the pathway for the Father in heaven to forgive us our own trespasses. Thus, forgiveness becomes an indispensable component of our spiritual walk, a reflection of the grace and mercy we have received from our Heavenly Father.

> *Mark 11:25 (ESV) And whenever you stand praying, forgive, if you have anything against anyone, so that your Father also who is in heaven may forgive you your trespasses."*

God, in His infinite love and mercy, sent His Son, Jesus Christ, to sacrifice Himself for our sins, thereby paving the way for our reconciliation with Him. In light of this profound act of forgiveness, God commands us to extend the same forgiveness to others, mirroring the grace we have received.

The essence of this command is beautifully illustrated in a parable shared by our Lord in Matthew 18:23-35. Although it's a lengthy passage, it holds invaluable lessons about the importance of forgiveness. It underscores the necessity of extending grace to others, as we ourselves have been recipients of God's boundless mercy. This parable serves as a sober reminder of the redemptive power of forgiveness and the profound impact it can have on our relationships and spiritual well-being.

> *Matthew 18:21-35 (ESV) Then Peter came up and said to him, "Lord, how often will my brother sin against me, and I forgive him? As many as seven times?" 22 Jesus said to him, "I do not say to you seven times, but seventy-seven times. 23 "Therefore the kingdom of heaven may be compared to a king who wished to settle accounts with his servants. 24 When he began to settle, one was brought to him who owed him ten thousand talents. 25 And since he could not pay, his master ordered him to be sold, with his wife and children and all that he had, and payment to be made. 26 So the servant fell on his knees, imploring him, 'Have patience with me, and I will pay you everything.' 27 And out of pity for him, the master of that servant released him and forgave him the debt. 28 But when that same servant went out, he found one of his fellow servants who owed him a hundred denarii, and seizing him, he began to choke him, saying, 'Pay what you owe.' 29 So his fellow servant fell down and pleaded with him, 'Have patience with me, and I will pay you.' 30 He refused and went and put him in prison until he should pay the debt. 31 When his fellow servants saw what had taken place, they were greatly distressed, and they went and reported to their master all that had taken place. 32 Then his master summoned him and said to him, 'You wicked servant! I forgave you all that debt because you pleaded with me. 33 And should not you have had mercy on your fellow servant, as I had mercy on you?' 34 And in anger his master delivered him to the jailers, until he should pay all his debt. 35 So also my*

heavenly Father will do to every one of you, if you do not forgive your brother from your heart."

Unforgiveness Shows We Don't Love Jesus Or Believe God In His Word.

Unforgiveness serves as a tangible indication that our love for Jesus and our trust in God's Word are not genuine. While we may claim to love the Lord outwardly, our actions speak volumes about the true state of our hearts. Walking in unforgiveness distances us from God, regardless of the words we profess with our lips. The fruit of our lives invariably exposes the root of our faith.

Jesus himself emphasized the inseparable connection between love for Him and obedience to His commandments. This principle is eloquently articulated in John 15:12, where Jesus instructs His disciples to love one another just as He has loved them. This verse captures the essence of genuine love for Christ, which is demonstrated through our willingness to follow His teachings and extend forgiveness to others.

> *John 15:12 (ESV) "This is my commandment, that you love one another as I have loved you.*
>
> *John 14:15 (ESV) "If you love me, you will keep my commandments.*

We Are Forgiven Directly Proportional To Us Forgiving

Within Christianity, there exists a tendency towards the concept of blanket forgiveness—a convenient notion that allows believers to readily receive forgiveness for their actions without genuine repentance or transformation. This inclination is often intertwined with the notion of easy believism, wherein individuals perceive salvation as a simple transaction, marked by a brief prayer and subsequent freedom to live according to personal desires. However, this distorted view of salvation lacks the essential element of repentance and genuine faith, which fails to produce meaningful life change.

Similarly, when it comes to forgiveness, many believers seek a quick fix—a blanket forgiveness that absolves them of any wrongdoing without requiring sincere repentance or acknowledgment of their actions. We've all heard prayers along the lines of, "Lord, forgive me if I have sinned today," or the sweeping request at day's end, "Lord, forgive me of all my many sins." Yet, all too often, even as these prayers are uttered, individuals harbor unforgiveness towards others in their hearts.

This reveals a critical disconnection between the outward expression of faith and the internal transformation that true salvation and forgiveness should contain. Genuine salvation and forgiveness are not mere rituals or superficial declarations; they are transformative experiences that reshape hearts, minds, and actions, leading to a life characterized by authentic faith and love.

As we delve into the Scriptures concerning forgiveness, a clear principle emerges: the measure of forgiveness we extend to others directly influences the forgiveness we receive from God. This reciprocal relationship underscores the profound impact of forgiveness on our spiritual well-being.

Unforgiveness, in its essence, acts as a barrier to God's forgiveness of our own sins. When we cling to bitterness and resentment towards others, we create a barrier that inhibits the flow of God's mercy and grace into our lives. This truth is evident throughout Scripture, highlighting the inseparable connection between our willingness to forgive and our ability to receive forgiveness from God.

Therefore, forgiveness operates as a two-way street — a divine exchange where our capacity to forgive mirrors the depth of God's forgiveness towards us. It underscores the transformative power of forgiveness in restoring relationships, healing wounds, and ultimately, drawing us closer to the heart of God. There you have it. So much for the false "blanket forgiveness" theology mentality we have received from our spiritual leaders.

> *Matthew 6:12 (ESV) and forgive us our debts, as we also have forgiven our debtors.*
>
> *Matthew 6:14-15 (ESV) For if you forgive others their trespasses, your heavenly Father will also forgive you, 15 but if you do not forgive others their trespasses, neither will your Father forgive your trespasses.*
>
> *Mark 11:25 (ESV) And whenever you stand praying, forgive, if you have anything against anyone, so that your Father also who is in heaven may forgive you your trespasses."*
>
> *Luke 6:37 (ESV) "Judge not, and you will not be judged; condemn not, and you will not be condemned; forgive, and you will be forgiven;*
>
> *Luke 11:4 (ESV) and forgive us our sins, for we ourselves forgive everyone who is indebted to us. And lead us not into temptation."*

Ephesians 4:32 (ESV) Be kind to one another, tenderhearted, forgiving one another, as God in Christ forgave you.

Colossians 3:12-13 (ESV) Put on then, as God's chosen ones, holy and beloved, compassionate hearts, kindness, humility, meekness, and patience, 13 bearing with one another and, if one has a complaint against another, forgiving each other; as the Lord has forgiven you, so you also must forgive.

The Dangers Of Unforgiveness:

Unforgiveness exposes us to the tormentors, who are representative of the demonic and their influence in our lives. The full narrative in Matthew 18:23-35 provides profound insight into the consequences of harboring unforgiveness.

In this passage, our Lord Jesus Christ shares a parable about a servant who owed an enormous debt to his master. Despite the servant's inability to repay, the master, moved by compassion, forgave the entire debt. However, when the same servant encountered a fellow servant who owed him a much smaller sum, he refused to extend the same grace and compassion, instead choosing to demand payment, and even resorting to harsh treatment.

The master, upon learning of this injustice, revoked his forgiveness and handed the unforgiving servant over to the tormentors until he could repay his debt in full. This parable serves as a sobering reminder of the consequences of unforgiveness in our lives. When we refuse to forgive others, we inadvertently invite torment and bondage into our own lives, allowing the enemy to gain a foothold.

By studying this parable, we gain insight into the importance of extending forgiveness to others, not only for their sake but also for our own spiritual and physical well-being. It underscores the need to release the burdens of bitterness and resentment, allowing the power of God's forgiveness to bring healing and freedom to our hearts and relationships.

> *Matthew 18:23 (ESV) "Therefore the kingdom of heaven may be compared to a king who wished to settle accounts with his servants.*
>
> *Matthew 18:27 (ESV) And out of pity for him, the master of that servant released him and forgave him the debt.*
>
> *Matthew 18:32-35 (ESV) Then his master summoned him and said to him, 'You wicked servant! I forgave you all that debt because you pleaded with me. 33 And should not you have had mercy on your fellow servant, as I had mercy on you?' 34 And in anger his master delivered him to the jailers, until he should pay all his debt. 35 So also my heavenly Father will do to every one of you, if you do not forgive your brother from your heart."*

Unforgiveness Can Block God From Answering Our Prayers.

As believers, our hearts long for the assurance that our prayers are heard and answered by God. It becomes our solemn responsibility to actively address any potential barriers that might obstruct the flow of our prayers from reaching God's ears and receiving His response. Among these barriers, unforgiveness stands as a formidable obstacle that can hinder the effectiveness of our prayers.

Unforgiveness possesses the power to create a barrier between us and God, preventing our prayers from reaching His throne of grace. When we harbor unforgiveness in our hearts, we allow bitterness, resentment, and unresolved conflicts to take root, creating a spiritual blockage that disrupts our connection with God.

This truth emphasizes the importance of cultivating a spirit of forgiveness in our lives. By releasing grudges, extending grace, and seeking reconciliation with others, we actively dismantle the barriers of unforgiveness that hinder our prayers from being heard and answered. In doing so, we open wide the channels of communication with God, creating a pathway for our prayers to ascend before Him and receive His attentive and gracious response. Thus, embracing forgiveness becomes not only a hallmark of our faith but also a vital component in the realization of answered prayers and deepened communion with our Heavenly Father.

> *Isaiah 59:1-2 (ESV) Behold, the LORD's hand is not shortened, that it cannot save, or his ear dull, that it cannot hear; 2 but your iniquities have made a separation between you and your God, and your sins have hidden his face from you so that he does not hear.*
>
> *Mark 11:24-25 (ESV) Therefore I tell you, whatever you ask in prayer, believe that you have received it, and it will be yours. 25 And whenever you stand praying, forgive, if you have anything against anyone, so that your Father also who is in heaven may forgive you your trespasses."*

BE HEALED

Unforgiveness Can Give Satan An Advantage.

Recall the situation in 1 Corinthians 5 where Paul sternly addressed the Corinthian church for tolerating sexual immorality among its members. In response, he instructed the church to remove the guilty individual from their fellowship, implementing a form of discipline known as excommunication. The directive was clear: sever all ties with the offending person and exclude them from the church community.

> *1 Corinthians 5:1-2 (ESV) It is actually reported that there is sexual immorality among you, and of a kind that is not tolerated even among pagans, for a man has his father's wife. 2 And you are arrogant! Ought you not rather to mourn? Let him who has done this be removed from among you.*

In 2 Corinthians 2:5-11, Paul addresses the Corinthian believers, informing them that the individual in question has expressed genuine repentance. Consequently, Paul urges the church to extend forgiveness and readmit the individual into their fellowship. He emphasizes the importance of avoiding unforgiveness, as it leaves the church vulnerable to the schemes of the enemy.

> *2 Corinthians 2:5-11 (ESV) Now if anyone has caused pain, he has caused it not to me, but in some measure—not to put it too severely—to all of you. 6 For such a one, this punishment by the majority is enough, 7 so you should rather turn to forgive and comfort him, or he may be overwhelmed by excessive sorrow. 8 So I beg you to reaffirm your love for him. 9*

> *For this is why I wrote, that I might test you and know whether you are obedient in everything. 10 Anyone whom you forgive, I also forgive. Indeed, what I have forgiven, if I have forgiven anything, has been for your sake in the presence of Christ, 11 so that we would not be outwitted by Satan; for we are not ignorant of his designs.*

Unforgiveness Can Prevent Us From Being Fruitful Spiritually.

Unforgiveness has the potential to hinder our spiritual growth and productivity in profound ways. Like we said earlier, when we hold onto grudges, resentments, and bitterness towards others, it creates a barrier within our hearts that obstructs the flow of God's grace and blessings into our lives.

Spiritual fruitfulness is deeply intertwined with our ability to extend forgiveness and reconcile with those who have wronged us. Unforgiveness stifles the work of the Holy Spirit within us, preventing us from experiencing the fullness of God's love, joy, peace, patience, kindness, goodness, faithfulness, gentleness, and self-control.

When we walk in the Spirit, the fruit of the Holy Spirit becomes evident in our lives. However, unforgiveness hinders our ability to walk in the Spirit. Instead, it leads us to walk in the flesh, where we are more likely to engage in the sinful deeds associated with the flesh.

> *Galatians 5:16 (ESV) But I say, walk by the Spirit, and you will not gratify the desires of the flesh.*

Unforgiveness disrupts our relationships with others, causing division, strife, and discord within the body of

Christ. It impedes our ability to bear witness to the redemptive power of God's love and grace in our lives.

Basically, unforgiveness not only inhibits our spiritual growth and effectiveness but also hinders the manifestation of God's kingdom purposes in and through us. Therefore, it is imperative that we cultivate a spirit of forgiveness, seeking reconciliation and restoration in all our relationships, so that we may bear abundant fruit for the glory of God.

> *John 15:4-7 (ESV) Abide in me, and I in you. As the branch cannot bear fruit by itself, unless it abides in the vine, neither can you, unless you abide in me. 5 I am the vine; you are the branches. Whoever abides in me and I in him, he it is that bears much fruit, for apart from me you can do nothing. 6 If anyone does not abide in me he is thrown away like a branch and withers; and the branches are gathered, thrown into the fire, and burned. 7 If you abide in me, and my words abide in you, ask whatever you wish, and it will be done for you.*

Unforgiveness Can Open Us Up To Curses.

Unforgiveness carries the potential to invite curses into our lives. Throughout the Old Testament, when individuals disobeyed God's commandments, they often found themselves subject to curses as a consequence. Similarly, in modern times, disobedience to God's teachings can expose individuals to similar outcomes, potentially inviting curses into their lives.

These curses, when unleashed, can manifest in various forms, including mental and emotional distress. They may bring about turmoil, unrest, and inner conflict, impacting one's mental and emotional well-being profoundly. Thus, harboring unforgiveness not only disrupts our relationship and fellowship with others but also leaves us vulnerable to the adverse spiritual and physical consequences that may follow. Deuteronomy gives us a breakdown of curses released through disobedience to God's laws. (Read Deuteronomy 28:15-68)

> *Deuteronomy 27:26 (ESV) "'Cursed be anyone who does not confirm the words of this law by doing them.' And all the people shall say, 'Amen.'*

Forgiveness And Healing

> *1 John 4:7-8 (ESV) Beloved, let us love one another, for love is from God, and whoever loves has been born of God and knows God. 8 Anyone who does not love does not know God, because God is love.*

As stated in 1 John 4:7-8, love originates from God, for He embodies love in its purest form. This love not only defines God's character but also serves as a model for how we should live our lives. In alignment with this principle, we are called to center our lives around the concept of forgiveness, mirroring God's own forgiveness towards us.

Ephesians 4:31-32 outlines the transformative power of forgiveness in our lives. It exhorts us to discard negative emotions such as bitterness, rage, anger, quarreling, and slander, along with every form of malice. Instead, we are encouraged to embrace qualities such as kindness and compassion, extending forgiveness to one another just as God, through Christ, has forgiven us.

BE HEALED

> *Ephesians 4:31-32 (ESV) Let all bitterness and wrath and anger and clamor and slander be put away from you, along with all malice. 32 Be kind to one another, tenderhearted, forgiving one another, as God in Christ forgave you.*

This passage serves as a sober reminder of our Lord's redemptive power of salvation and forgiveness. By releasing bitterness and embracing compassion, we mirror the forgiveness extended to us by God through the sacrifice of Christ. In doing so, we not only experience personal transformation but also foster a culture of grace, reconciliation, and love within our Christian communities. Paul pleaded with the church to forgive the man who had been cast out.

> *2 Corinthians 2:5-11 (ESV) Now if anyone has caused pain, he has caused it not to me, but in some measure—not to put it too severely—to all of you. 6 For such a one, this punishment by the majority is enough, 7 so you should rather turn to forgive and comfort him, or he may be overwhelmed by excessive sorrow. 8 So I beg you to reaffirm your love for him. 9 For this is why I wrote, that I might test you and know whether you are obedient in everything. 10 Anyone whom you forgive, I also forgive. Indeed, what I have forgiven, if I have forgiven anything, has been for your sake in the presence of Christ, 11 so that we would not be outwitted by Satan; for we are not ignorant of his designs.*

Throughout both the Old and New Testaments, forgiveness emerges as a central aspect of God's character in His interactions with humanity. Numerous instances highlight God's profound capacity for forgiveness, particularly exemplified in the life of Jesus Christ.

One of the most compelling examples of forgiveness is demonstrated in Jesus' compassionate response to the adulterous woman who faced stoning. In this story, Jesus extends grace and mercy, offering forgiveness and protection to the woman condemned by society. This act not only showcases Jesus' unwavering commitment to forgiveness but also highlights His redemptive and life-changing power of compassion and grace in the face of judgment and condemnation.

> *John 8:3-11 (ESV) The scribes and the Pharisees brought a woman who had been caught in adultery, and placing her in the midst 4 they said to him, "Teacher, this woman has been caught in the act of adultery. 5 Now in the Law, Moses commanded us to stone such women. So what do you say?" 6 This they said to test him, that they might have some charge to bring against him. Jesus bent down and wrote with his finger on the ground. 7 And as they continued to ask him, he stood up and said to them, "Let him who is without sin among you be the first to throw a stone at her." 8 And once more he bent down and wrote on the ground. 9 But when they heard it, they went away one by one, beginning with the older ones, and Jesus was left alone with the woman standing before him. 10 Jesus stood up and said to her, "Woman, where are they? Has no one condemned you?" 11 She said, "No one, Lord." And Jesus said, "Neither do I condemn you; go, and from now on sin no more."]]*

The entire story of Jesus' life, ministry, and ultimate sacrifice on the cross embodies the essence of forgiveness, serving as a profound testament to God's boundless love and mercy towards humanity. As we reflect on these examples, we are invited to emulate God's forgiveness in our own lives, extending grace and compassion to others as a reflection of His eternal love.

Jesus On The Cross:

During one of the most agonizing moments in human history, as Jesus hung on the cross, He uttered a profound plea to His heavenly Father: "Forgive them, for they do not know what they are doing." In this remarkable act of forgiveness, even in the face of excruciating pain and injustice, Jesus exemplified the boundless compassion and mercy of God.

> Luke 23:34 (ESV) And Jesus said, "Father, forgive them, for they know not what they do." And they cast lots to divide his garments.

In extending forgiveness, we witness a profound manifestation of God's character. It is through forgiveness that the transformative power of God's love becomes real, offering a pathway to healing and reconciliation. When we choose to forgive, we reflect the divine nature of God Himself, embodying His grace and mercy in our interactions with others.

The act of forgiveness holds the capacity to heal wounds, restore relationships, and bring about profound inner transformation. It is a testament to the redemptive nature of God's love, offering a glimpse of His unending grace and compassion even in the midst of human frailty and brokenness.

As we contemplate the depth of Jesus' forgiveness on the cross, we are challenged to embrace forgiveness in our own lives, recognizing its potential and ability to reflect the character of God to a world in need of healing and reconciliation.

As children of God, our journey toward knowing the Father intimately leads us to increasingly reflect His character in our lives. Love and forgiveness gradually become intrinsic to our nature as we deepen our relationship with Him. However, this transformation is not always automatic or immediate. Our emotions, attitudes, and the circumstances we face often tempt us to respond in ways contrary to love and forgiveness.

Forgiveness, despite its challenges, serves as a powerful force for healing and restoration in the lives of those who have experienced hurt and pain. By extending forgiveness, we create space for God to intervene and work miracles in the hearts of both the forgiver and the forgiven. It is through forgiveness that the cycle of brokenness and resentment is broken, paving the way for reconciliation and spiritual growth.

Illness can profoundly impact both the mind and body, presenting alarming challenges to our emotional and physical well-being. In the face of illness, we are confronted with a choice: to succumb to despair and bitterness, or to cling to hope and trust in God's sovereignty.

Ultimately, our response to life's circumstances, whether it be forgiveness in the face of hurt or resilience in the midst of illness, reflects our commitment to aligning our lives with God's will. As we navigate the complexities of life, may we be guided by the Father's power of love, forgiveness, and faith, allowing Him to work His miracles in and through us, even in the midst of adversity.

BE HEALED

What Can We Do?

In wrapping up this discussion, it's crucial to acknowledge the significant relationship between sickness and sin. While there exists a connection between the two, the nature of this relationship varies significantly depending on individual circumstances. A comprehensive perspective recognizes the diversity of relationships between sickness and sin, considering the complexities inherent in each situation.

Sin, a universal reality in human experience, may or may not lead to sickness in individuals, affecting their body, soul, or spirit. While some contend that all sickness ultimately stems from sin, the Bible presents a more balanced view, acknowledging that not all sickness directly results from sin. The origins of illness are various and not always straightforward; they often involve factors beyond mere moral cause and effect. However, we do have a principle laid out in James 5:13-16 that we must take in account when dealing with the connection of sin and sickness. Confession of sin is paramount in our healing. In these Scriptures we see that healing is directly tied to our forgiveness.

> *James 5:13-16 (ESV) Is anyone among you suffering? Let him pray. Is anyone cheerful? Let him sing praise. 14 Is anyone among you sick? Let him call for the elders of the church, and let them pray over him, anointing him with oil in the name of the Lord. 15 And the prayer of faith will save the one who is sick, and the Lord will raise him up. And if he has committed sins, he will be forgiven. 16 Therefore, confess your sins to one another and pray for one*

another, that you may be healed. The prayer of a righteous person has great power as it is working.

Throughout history, sickness has been erroneously attributed to Satan and sometimes regarded as a divine punishment from God. However, such interpretations fail to capture the full complexity of illness and its origins. While God desires wholeness and health for His people, His primary concern lies in addressing the root cause of human suffering: A sinful heart caused by a sinful nature.

God's ultimate priority through the redemptive work of our Lord Jesus Christ, is the healing of our souls from sin, rather than just the physical healing of our bodies. While physical health is important, spiritual wholeness takes precedence in God's eyes. Therefore, as we grapple with the complexities of sickness and sin, may we seek God's guidance and grace, trusting in His sovereignty and His ultimate desire for our body, soul, and spirit be well.

Chapter 14
REAPING WHAT YOU SOW CAN CAUSE SICKNESS, ILLNESS, DISEASE, AND DEATH

Galatians 6:7-8, often referred to as *"The Law of Reaping and Sowing,"* captures a fundamental principle of spiritual and natural law. It underscores the concept that our actions yield consequences, akin to the seeds we sow in a field.

This principle aligns with the Genesis narrative where God brings forth animals, birds, fish, fruit, trees, and plants according to their own kind. It reflects the law of "like kind," where each organism reproduces after its own kind, maintaining the integrity of its species.

> *Galatians 6:7-8 (ESV) Do not be deceived: God is not mocked, for whatever one sows, that will he also reap. 8 For the one who sows to his own flesh will from the flesh reap corruption, but the one who sows to the Spirit will from the Spirit reap eternal life.*

> *Genesis 1:21 (ESV) So God created the great sea creatures and every living creature that moves, with which the waters swarm, according to their kinds, and every winged bird according to its kind. And God saw that it was good.*

> *Genesis 1:25 (ESV) And God made the beasts of the earth according to their kinds and the livestock according to their kinds, and everything that creeps on the ground according to its kind. And God saw that it was good.*

Genesis 6:20 (ESV) Of the birds according to their kinds, and of the animals according to their kinds, of every creeping thing of the ground, according to its kind, two of every sort shall come in to you to keep them alive.

Genesis 7:14 (ESV) they and every beast, according to its kind, and all the livestock according to their kinds, and every creeping thing that creeps on the earth, according to its kind, and every bird, according to its kind, every winged creature.

An example that would serve as a tangible illustration of this principle would be lung cancer in individuals who have smoked for many years.

In the context of smoking and lung cancer, the prolonged exposure to harmful substances found in cigarettes can significantly increase the risk of developing cancerous growths within the lungs. The seeds represented by the tobacco use is sown into the lungs with the potential for grave health consequences, and over time, this detrimental habit may culminate in the manifestation of serious illnesses like lung cancer.

This principle extends beyond the realm of physical health to encompass various aspects of human experience. Just as farmers reap what they sow in their fields, so too do individuals harvest the fruits of their actions. Whether in matters of health, relationships, or personal development, our choices and behaviors inevitably shape the outcomes we experience.

If I inflict significant harm upon someone that leads to my incarceration, God may forgive me for the sins of physical, mental, and emotional damage I caused. However, the consequences of my actions may still manifest in the form of imprisonment. Despite receiving forgiveness for the wrongdoing, the repercussions of my behavior, such as legal ramifications and imprisonment, remain tangible outcomes that I must face and accept.

Galatians 6:7-8 serves as a sobering reminder of the importance of intentional living and mindful decision-making. It prompts us to consider the seeds we are sowing in our lives and the potential ramifications of our actions. By embracing wisdom, discernment, and accountability, we can navigate life's complexities with greater clarity and purpose, endeavoring to sow seeds of righteousness and reap a harvest of blessings in due time.

Continuously engaging in personal sins sets a process in motion where the seeds we sow yield a corresponding harvest. As we said, this fundamental principle is often referred to as "*The Law of Reaping and Sowing.*"

Many believers may readily embrace the promises of blessings outlined in passages like the "Blessing of Jabez" in 1 Chronicles 4:9-10 and the blessings of Deuteronomy 28:1-14. However, it's equally essential to consider the consequences of disobedience to God and His Word detailed in Deuteronomy 28:15-68. Persisting in personal sins is akin to cultivating a field of destruction, where the seeds of disobedience yield a harvest of adverse outcomes.

> *1 Chronicles 4:9-10 (ESV) Jabez was more honorable than his brothers; and his mother called his name Jabez, saying, "Because I bore him in pain." 10 Jabez called upon the God of Israel, saying, "Oh that you would bless me and enlarge my border, and that your hand might be with me, and that you would keep me from harm so that it might not bring me pain!" And God granted what he asked.*

Just as farmers reap what they sow in their fields, our actions and choices have corresponding consequences. The continuous indulgence in sinful behaviors plants seeds of destruction that eventually bear fruit in the form of negative repercussions and hardships. It's crucial for believers to recognize the gravity of their actions and strive to align their lives with God's principles and commands, knowing that obedience leads to blessings while disobedience leads to undesirable consequences. Jesus said that we are to follow Him.

> *Galatians 6:7-8 (ESV) Do not be deceived: God is not mocked, for whatever one sows, that will he also reap. 8 For the one who sows to his own flesh will from the flesh reap corruption, but the one who sows to the Spirit will from the Spirit reap eternal life.*

> *Psalms 107:17-20 (ESV) Some were fools through their sinful ways, and because of their iniquities suffered affliction; 18 they loathed any kind of food, and they drew near to the gates of death. 19 Then they cried to the LORD in their trouble, and he delivered them from their distress. 20 He sent out his word and healed them, and delivered them from their destruction.*

What Can We Do?

While exiled on the island of Patmos, the apostle John experienced a profound vision in which God granted him insight into the Revelation of Jesus Christ. Within this revelation, our Lord conveyed messages to the seven churches situated in Asian Minor. Among these messages, the Church of Ephesus received a command from the Lord: "remember, repent, and do."

> *Revelation 2:5 (ESV) Remember therefore from where you have fallen; repent, and do the works you did at first. If not, I will come to you and remove your lampstand from its place, unless you repent.*

The principle of reaping what one sows is a recurring theme throughout scripture. It underscores the notion that the consequences of our actions are directly correlated to the seeds we plant. Just as a farmer must plow up fallow ground and sow new crops to avoid reaping unwanted outcomes, individuals are encouraged to sow seeds of righteousness if they desire to harvest righteousness. Similarly, those seeking to cultivate health in their lives must actively sow seeds of health and well-being.

This principle, known as the law of reaping what you sow, emphasizes the importance of intentional living and mindful decision-making. By aligning our actions with our desired outcomes, we pave the way for the manifestation of blessings and prosperity in our lives. Conversely, neglecting to sow seeds of righteousness and health may result in an undesirable harvest. Therefore, let us be diligent in cultivating fields of righteousness, health, and spiritual growth, knowing that our efforts will yield a bountiful harvest in due time.

There you have it. The Biblical twelve ways someone faced sickness, illness, disease, and death and how they were healed.

1. *Personal Sins Can Cause Sickness, Illness, Disease. And Death.*

2. Sins Of The Forefathers Can Cause Sickness, Illness, Disease And Death.
3. Word Curses Can Cause Sickness, Illness, Disease, And Death.
4. Ungodly Soul Ties Can Cause Sickness, Illness, Disease, And Death.
5. Demonic Presence In Way Of Oppression Or Possession Can Cause Sickness, Illness, Disease, And Death.
6. Natural Law Of Sin And Death Can Cause Sickness, Illness, Disease And Death.
7. Sickness, Illness, Disease, And Death Can Come Upon Us For God's Glory To Be Manifested.
8. Judgment Of The Flesh For The Purpose Of Reconciliation Can Cause Sickness, Illness, Disease, And Death.
9. Taking The Lord's Supper In An Unworthy Manner Can Cause Sickness, Illness, Disease, And Death.
10. Lying To The Holy Spirit Can Cause Sickness, Illness, Disease, And Death.
11. Unforgiveness Can Cause Sickness, Illness, Disease, And Death.
12. Reaping What You Sow Can Cause Sickness, Illness, Disease, And Death.

Chapter 15
KEYS TO FOLLOW FOR HEALING

We have explored twelve instances where sickness befell individuals according to the Word of God. Following each explanation of the causes of sickness and ailments, we provided a call to action titled "What Can We Do?" It's important to remember that Romans 10:17 reminds us that faith is generated through hearing, and hearing is derived from the Word of God. With that in mind, I will now share healing Scriptures to invigorate faith within your soul and spirit. Take the time to read these Scriptures aloud, allowing the power of the Word to resonate within you as you meditate on its promises regarding healing. Remember that God is our healer, and the Scriptures say that by the stripes of our Lord Jesus Christ we are healed.

> *Romans 10:17 (ESV) So faith comes from hearing, and hearing through the word of Christ.*
>
> *Jeremiah 17:14 (ESV) Heal me, O LORD, and I shall be healed; save me, and I shall be saved, for you are my praise.*
>
> *Psalms 30:2 (ESV) O LORD my God, I cried to you for help, and you have healed me.*
>
> *Isaiah 53:5 (ESV) But he was pierced for our transgressions; he was crushed for our iniquities; upon him was the chastisement that brought us peace, and with his wounds we are healed.*

Matthew 8:17 (ESV) This was to fulfill what was spoken by the prophet Isaiah: "He took our illnesses and bore our diseases."

I want to emphasize that the list of healing Scriptures provided here is by no means exhaustive. Additionally, I may not have included every Scripture that could shed light on each point discussed. Consider this compilation as a foundational starting point for delving into the topic of "sicknesses versus healings." Despite the varied reasons for sickness or ailment, there are common principles underlying the healing process that I'd like to highlight. These basic steps towards healing can serve as a guide, regardless of the specific circumstances or causes of illness.

Examples Of Healing Based On The Faith Of Others

- *The centurion's servant in Luke 7:1-10.*
- *The resurrection of the daughter of Jairus in Luke 8:41-55.*
- *The pleading for Lazarus to be healed and yet died, only to be raised in John 11:1-43.*
- *The healing of the man with palsy in Luke 5:17-26.*

It's important to note that in these instances, Jesus observed THEIR FAITH—highlighting the healings that stemmed from the intercession and faith of loved ones, rather than solely relying on the faith and personal walk of the sick individual.

Examples Of Healing Based On Obedience To God's Word

BE HEALED

Proverbs 4:20-23 (ESV) My son, be attentive to my words; incline your ear to my sayings. 21 Let them not escape from your sight; keep them within your heart. 22 For they are life to those who find them, and healing to all their flesh. 23 Keep your heart with all vigilance, for from it flow the springs of life.

- *Pay attention to God's Word. (4:20)*
- *Listen closely to what He says. (4:20)*
- *Keep God's Word before you. (4:21)*
- *Keep God's Word in your mind and heart. (4:21)*
- *Believe the promise (4:22)*
- *Guard your heart (4:23)*

Exodus 15:26 (ESV) saying, "If you will diligently listen to the voice of the LORD your God, and do that which is right in his eyes, and give ear to his commandments and keep all his statutes, I will put none of the diseases on you that I put on the Egyptians, for I am the LORD, your healer."

- *Listen closely to what God says. (15:26)*
- *Do what is right in HIS sight. (15:26)*
- *Keep God's Word before you. (15:26)*
- *Keep God's laws. (15:26)*

Exodus 23:25-27 (ESV) You shall serve the LORD your God, and he will bless your bread and your water, and I will take sickness away from among you. 26 None shall miscarry or be barren in your land; I will fulfill the number of your days. 27 I will send my terror before you and will throw into confusion all the people against whom you shall come, and I will make all your enemies turn their backs to you.

- *God blesses our needs as we serve Him. (23:25)*
- *As we worship Him, He removes our ailments. (23:25)*
- *None will miscarry. (23:26)*
- *You will live a FULL LIFE span. (23:26)*

Examples Of Healing Or Death Based On Individuals Or Nations Maintaining Faith, Belief, And The Word

> *Hebrews 4:5-6 (ESV) And again in this passage he said, "They shall not enter my rest." 6 Since therefore it remains for some to enter it, and those who formerly received the good news failed to enter because of disobedience,*
>
> *James 1:6-8 (ESV) But let him ask in faith, with no doubting, for the one who doubts is like a wave of the sea that is driven and tossed by the wind. 7 For that person must not suppose that he will receive anything from the Lord; 8 he is a double-minded man, unstable in all his ways.*
>
> *Numbers 23:19-20 (ESV) God is not man, that he should lie, or a son of man, that he should change his mind. Has he said, and will he not do it? Or has he spoken, and will he not fulfill it? 20 Behold, I received a command to bless: he has blessed, and I cannot revoke it.*
>
> *1 Kings 8:56-57 (ESV) "Blessed be the LORD who has given rest to his people Israel, according to all that he promised. Not one word has failed of all his good promise, which he spoke by Moses his servant. 57 The LORD our God be with us, as he was with our fathers. May he not leave us or forsake us,*

BE HEALED

Psalms 119:87-92 (ESV) They have almost made an end of me on earth, but I have not forsaken your precepts. 88 In your steadfast love give me life, that I may keep the testimonies of your mouth. 89 Lamedh Forever, O LORD, your word is firmly fixed in the heavens. 90 Your faithfulness endures to all generations; you have established the earth, and it stands fast. 91 By your appointment they stand this day, for all things are your servants. 92 If your law had not been my delight, I would have perished in my affliction.

Isaiah 55:10-11 (ESV) "For as the rain and the snow come down from heaven and do not return there but water the earth, making it bring forth and sprout, giving seed to the sower and bread to the eater, 11 so shall my word be that goes out from my mouth; it shall not return to me empty, but it shall accomplish that which I purpose, and shall succeed in the thing for which I sent it.

The Supernatural Gifts Of Healing

This teaching on the Gifts of Healing is quite radical. Due to the necessary "faith issue" involved, many may dismiss this teaching. Embracing this gift prompts us to confront the "crisis of faith" on a daily basis. It's often convenient to claim, "The sick person lacked the faith to be healed." It's also convenient to assert, "If it is God's will, you will be healed."

Let's delve into the responsibility of the individual who prays for healing and who stands as the conduit for releasing the "Gifts of Healing." It's crucial to explore the Scriptures and deepen our understanding of these intriguing gifts of healings. Let us earnestly pray that the Father restores these gifts in your fellowship and your lives, empowering all of us to walk in greater faith and effectiveness in ministering healing to others.

Desire Spiritual Gifts: There Are Supernational Gifts Of Healing

> *1 Corinthians 14:1 (ESV) Pursue love, and earnestly desire the spiritual gifts, especially that you may prophesy.*
>
> *1 Corinthians 12:7-11 (ESV) To each is given the manifestation of the Spirit for the common good. 8 For to one is given through the Spirit the utterance of wisdom, and to another the utterance of knowledge according to the same Spirit, 9 to another faith by the same Spirit,* **to another gifts of healing by the one Spirit***, 10 to another the working of miracles, to another prophecy, to another the ability to distinguish between spirits, to another various kinds of tongues, to another the interpretation of tongues. 11 All these are empowered by one and the same Spirit, who apportions to each one individually as he wills.*

What are the spiritual gifts of healing? How are they recognized? Are they for today? How are they exercised? Gifts of Healing are sovereign supernatural manifestations of the Holy Spirit and not gifts of man.

> *1 Corinthians 12:11 (ESV) All these are empowered by one and the same Spirit, who apportions to each one individually as he wills.*

In 1 Corinthians 12:11, we learn that all spiritual gifts are empowered by the same Spirit, who distributes them individually according to His will. The Holy Spirit bestows gifts as He sees fit, choosing those whom He deems suitable. There are no specific guidelines or passages that instruct us on how to acquire these gifts independently. They cannot be earned or deserved through human effort.

Although gifts may be imparted through the practice of "laying on of hands," it is crucial to recognize that it is ultimately the will and purpose of the Holy Spirit that is being fulfilled. The act of laying on of hands serves as a means through which the Holy Spirit's divine will is manifested, rather than a method for individuals to manipulate or acquire gifts on their own accord. It underscores the sovereignty and wisdom of the Spirit in bestowing gifts according to His divine plan and purpose.

Not Everyone Will Be Used With The Manifested Gifts Of Healing Gift.

> *1 Corinthians 12:28-30 (ESV) And God has appointed in the church first apostles, second prophets, third teachers, then miracles, **then gifts of healing**, helping, administrating, and various kinds of tongues. 29 Are all apostles? Are all prophets? Are all teachers? Do all work miracles? 30 Do all possess gifts of healing? Do all speak with tongues? Do all interpret?*

When we see the Gifts of Healing in operation in the Church today it should be as the New Testament example.

- *It was more dependent upon the healer than upon the sick person. This does not take the responsibility from the sick person, but it adds to the fact that it is the praying person walking in the Holy Spirit who initiates*

healing. (Acts 3:6, 5:15-16, 9:40, 14:3, 16:18, 19:11-12)
- *It had more immediate and permanent results instead of the short-term healings and the long periods of waiting for prayer results.*
- *The Gifts of healing follow those who follow after the heart of the Father. (Acts 3:12, 8:6, 14:3, Mark 16:20)*
- *When God releases the Gifts of healing, there are no failures. (Acts 5:16, Matthew 8:16)*
- *When God releases the Gifts of healing, the sickness and the healing was obvious to everyone. (Acts 3:2, 5:15, 8:7, 9:37, 14:8)*

The Faith Of The One Afflicted

Consider the faith of the individual who is sick. While some experienced healing through their own faith, it was often intertwined with the faith of the one acting as the healer. Healing can indeed occur when the faith of the sick person aligns with the faith of the healer. However, healing typically doesn't manifest solely through the faith of the sick individual; it necessitates the presence of faith in the healer as well.

> *Acts 14:8-10 (ESV) Now at Lystra there was a man sitting who could not use his feet. He was crippled from birth and had never walked. 9 He listened to Paul speaking. And Paul, looking intently at him and seeing that he had faith to be made well, 10 said in a loud voice, "Stand upright on your feet." And he sprang up and began walking.*

In Acts 14:8-10, the passage doesn't explicitly state that the man's faith was the sole factor in his healing. Rather, it indicates that he possessed faith that healing was possible.

BE HEALED

Many individuals have faith in the potential for healing, yet they often require someone with the faith to pray and intercede as the healer.

Consider the scenario of praying for a lost person. Should we tell them they lack faith for healing? Numerous lost individuals approached Jesus seeking healing, yet it was His divine gifting, coupled with faith, that brought about their healing. Lost individuals are endowed with a measure of faith to accept Jesus as their Savior, but it's questionable whether they possess faith specifically for physical healing. Such faith appears to be associated with believers who have accepted Jesus Christ as their Lord and Savior.

> *Matthew 17:14-20 (ESV) And when they came to the crowd, a man came up to him and, kneeling before him, 15 said, "Lord, have mercy on my son, for he has seizures and he suffers terribly. For often he falls into the fire, and often into the water. 16 And I brought him to your disciples, and they could not heal him." 17 And Jesus answered, "O faithless and twisted generation, how long am I to be with you? How long am I to bear with you? Bring him here to me." 18 And Jesus rebuked the demon, and it came out of him, and the boy was healed instantly. 19 Then the disciples came to Jesus privately and said, "Why could we not cast it out?" 20 He said to them, **"Because of your little faith.** For truly, I say to you, if you have faith like a grain of mustard seed, you will say to this mountain, 'Move from here to there,' and it will move, and nothing will be impossible for you."*

In Matthew 17:14-20, we encounter a scenario where the Apostles attempted to heal someone but were unsuccessful. The failure to heal was not due to a deficiency in faith on the part of the sick individual, but rather a lack of faith among the healers themselves as stated in verse 20.

Anointing Someone With Oil

The word "CHIRO" means "To Anoint" and "CHRIST" means "The Anointed One."

> Luke 4:18 (ESV) "The Spirit of the Lord is upon me, because he has anointed me to proclaim good news to the poor. He has sent me to proclaim liberty to the captives and recovering of sight to the blind, to set at liberty those who are oppressed,

This is the same word used for a hair cosmetic or hair washing.

> Matthew 6:16-18 (ESV) "And when you fast, do not look gloomy like the hypocrites, for they disfigure their faces that their fasting may be seen by others. Truly, I say to you, they have received their reward. 17 But when you fast, anoint your head and wash your face, 18 that your fasting may not be seen by others but by your Father who is in secret. And your Father who sees in secret will reward you.

This is the same word used rubbing the body for burial.

> Mark 16:1 (ESV) When the Sabbath was past, Mary Magdalene, Mary the mother of James, and Salome bought spices, so that they might go and anoint him.

This is the same word used for rubbing the feet with oil.

BE HEALED

Luke 7:37-46 (ESV) And behold, a woman of the city, who was a sinner, when she learned that he was reclining at table in the Pharisee's house, brought an alabaster flask of ointment, 38 and standing behind him at his feet, weeping, she began to wet his feet with her tears and wiped them with the hair of her head and kissed his feet and anointed them with the ointment. 39 Now when the Pharisee who had invited him saw this, he said to himself, "If this man were a prophet, he would have known who and what sort of woman this is who is touching him, for she is a sinner." 40 And Jesus answering said to him, "Simon, I have something to say to you." And he answered, "Say it, Teacher." 41 "A certain moneylender had two debtors. One owed five hundred denarii, and the other fifty. 42 When they could not pay, he cancelled the debt of both. Now which of them will love him more?" 43 Simon answered, "The one, I suppose, for whom he cancelled the larger debt." And he said to him, "You have judged rightly." 44 Then turning toward the woman he said to Simon, "Do you see this woman? I entered your house; you gave me no water for my feet, but she has wet my feet with her tears and wiped them with her hair. 45 You gave me no kiss, but from the time I came in she has not ceased to kiss my feet. 46 You did not anoint my head with oil, but she has anointed my feet with ointment.

This is the same word used for rubbing or wiped.

John 11:2 (ESV) It was Mary who anointed the Lord with ointment and wiped his feet with her hair, whose brother Lazarus was ill.

> *James 5:14-15 (ESV) Is anyone among you sick? Let him call for the elders of the church, and let them pray over him, anointing him with oil in the name of the Lord. 15 And the prayer of faith will save the one who is sick, and the Lord will raise him up. And if he has committed sins, he will be forgiven.*

Those Who Are Sick Are Not Always Healed.

Epaphroditus

> *Philippians 2:25-30 (ESV) I have thought it necessary to send to you Epaphroditus my brother and fellow worker and fellow soldier, and your messenger and minister to my need, 26 for he has been longing for you all and has been distressed because you heard that he was ill. 27 Indeed he was ill, near to death. But God had mercy on him, and not only on him but on me also, lest I should have sorrow upon sorrow. 28 I am the more eager to send him, therefore, that you may rejoice at seeing him again, and that I may be less anxious. 29 So receive him in the Lord with all joy, and honor such men, 30 for he nearly died for the work of Christ, risking his life to complete what was lacking in your service to me.*

Trophimus

> *2 Timothy 4:20 (ESV) Erastus remained at Corinth, and I left Trophimus, who was ill, at Miletus.*

Paul

> *2 Corinthians 12:7-10 (ESV) So to keep me from becoming conceited because of the surpassing*

greatness of the revelations, a thorn was given me in the flesh, a messenger of Satan to harass me, to keep me from becoming conceited. 8 Three times I pleaded with the Lord about this, that it should leave me. 9 But he said to me, "My grace is sufficient for you, for my power is made perfect in weakness." Therefore I will boast all the more gladly of my weaknesses, so that the power of Christ may rest upon me. 10 For the sake of Christ, then, I am content with weaknesses, insults, hardships, persecutions, and calamities. For when I am weak, then I am strong.

Closing Thoughts

We acknowledge the healing power found in our Lord Jesus Christ. However, it's important to recognize that physical, emotional, or mental healing is not intended to be an ultimate destination in itself.

Healing the sick is a topic that carries profound significance and responsibility within the realm of faith and spirituality. As we reflect on this subject, several key insights and considerations emerge.

It's essential to acknowledge that healing is a complex process that involves various factors, including faith, prayer, fasting, divine intervention, and human agency. While faith plays a pivotal role in healing, it's not the only contributing factor. Prayer and being moved with compassionate care also play crucial roles in the Father's supernatural healing process.

We must recognize that healing manifests in diverse ways. While physical healing is often the focus, especially in prayer meetings, healing encompasses the restoration of the mind, body, and spirit. Emotional and spiritual healing are equally important aspects of the healing process and require our attention.

The pursuit of healing demands humility, compassion, and sensitivity. We must approach those who are sick and afflicted with compassion, empathy, understanding, and a genuine desire to alleviate their suffering. Praying over the sick should not be perceived merely as another religious task checked off our list for the week.

When preparing to enter a pray ministry time for the sick and afflicted we must listen attentively to the Holy Spirit to discern why the sickness is present and how to approach the healing process. The use of this spiritual wisdom can make a significant difference in someone's healing journey and lesson the stress of being ineffective in our prayers.

It's essential to maintain a posture of openness and receptivity to the guidance and power of the Holy Spirit. As we engage in prayers for healing, we must remain attuned to God's leading and discern His will for each situation. Trusting in God's sovereignty and wisdom allows us to surrender our desires and outcomes to His divine plan.

We must guard against oversimplifying the complexities of healing or placing undue pressure on individuals who are sick and afflicted. While we are called to pray for healing and exercise faith, we must also acknowledge that healing may not always occur in the manner or timing we expect. Embracing a posture of trust and surrender to our Lord Jesus Christ and the Holy Spirit enables us to navigate the uncertainties of the healing process with grace and resilience.

BE HEALED

1 Thessalonians 5:23 (ESV) Now may the God of peace himself sanctify you completely, and may your whole spirit and soul and body be kept blameless at the coming of our Lord Jesus Christ.

3 John 1:2 (ESV) Beloved, I pray that all may go well with you and that you may be in good health, as it goes well with your soul.

MORE BOOKS BY CHARLES MORRIS

1. The Four Positions Of The Holy Spirit
2. Born Again
3. The 10 Characteristics Of A Spirit-Filled Church
4. The Covenant Of Salt
5. The Parable Of The Four Soils
6. The Five Evidences Of Salvation
7. Hosea
8. Fifteen Ways To Hear The Voice Of God
9. The 24 Qualifications Of An Elder
10. The Bible Proves Itself True
11. Experiencing The Beauty Of Brokenness
12. Places Where God And Man Meet
13. Your Dash
14. Chart Your Path
15. The Five Witnesses Of Salvation
16. How Do I Write A Book?
17. Hosea Introduction
18. Hosea 1:1-3
19. Hosea 1:4-5
20. Hosea 1:6-7
21. Hosea 1:8-9
22. Hosea 1:10-11
23. A Willingness To Be Taught
24. Luke 15
25. The Chronological Book Of End Times
26. Is Atheism Dead?
27. Wherever You Go Travel Journal Adults
28. Wherever You Go Travel Journal Teens
29. The Topical Journal Veterans
30. The Topical Journal Women
31. The Topical Journal Adults
32. Wherever You Go Travel Journal Men
33. The Topical Journal Men
34. Is Religion Dead?

35. Unleashed
36. I Feel Like I'm Losing My Faith
37. We Need Faith
38. Is Christian Immaturity Dead?
39. The Parable Of The Wheat And Tares
40. Go Tell It On The Mountain
41. The Cost Of Discipleship
42. The Gospel According To Luke
43. The Gospel According To Jesus
44. I Am Light & Dark Blue, Light & Dark Pink, Gold & Peach
45. Six Enemies Of Faith
46. The Six Dangerous Love Affairs?
47. Overcoming Fear
48. Don't Give The Enemy A Seat At Your Table
49. A Course In Miracles
50. Angels
51. The Holy Spirit; Do I Have To Speak In Tongues?
52. Host The Holy Ghost
53. Devotional Bible Series Volume 1: Defeating The Sin Within Me
54. Devotional Bible Series Volume 2: A Backsliding Heart
55. Devotional Bible Series Volume 3: Six Enemies Of Faith
56. Devotional Bible Series Volume 4: The Spiritual Man
57. Devotional Bible Series Volume 5: Intimate Deception: What Are The Six Dangerous Love Affairs?
58. Devotional Bible Series Volume 6: Setting Your Heart
59. Devotional Bible Series Volume 7: Dare To Pray
60. Just Give Me One More
61. Our Holy Treasure
62. Whisper

ABOUT THE AUTHOR

CHARLES MORRIS has a rich legacy spanning 49 years as a dedicated servant of God to the body of Christ. His diverse roles as a pastor, church planter, evangelist, house church coordinator, and prolific author of over 50 books have left a profound impact on countless lives.

As the visionary founder and CEO of RSI Ministry and Raising the Standard International Publishing, Pastor Charles remains committed to inspiring believers to walk in God's holiness through the power and presence of the Holy Spirit.

Passionate about living according to God's standards, he tirelessly calls the church to embody Christ's likeness in their daily lives in word, deed and thought. Pastor Charles firmly believes in the significance of genuine salvation, encouraging all believers to examine their lives through the lens of God's Word.

Currently residing in Navarre, Florida, Pastor Charles finds unwavering support and partnership in life with his beloved wife, Debra.

Made in United States
North Haven, CT
19 April 2025